# Wild Daisies from the Side of the Road

## A Collective Tribute to Maurice Kenny

Edited by Derek C. Maus and Donald J. McNutt

**2018**

Many Moons Press

Potsdam, NY

The editors wish to thank the following individuals for their support during the process of producing this volume (in addition, of course, to all of those whose works appear herein):

Charlotte Aldrich, Anne Alsina, Kevin Bertolero, Sarah Bodah, Holly Chambers, Pam Cullen, Cheryl Culotta, Christine Doran, James J. Donahue, Tim and Diana Fortune, Demian and Lynx French, Alice Gilborn, Jeanette Godreau, Joy Harjo, Carolyn Hotaling, Jim and Mary Hotaling, Katarzyna Jerzak, Penelope Kelsey, Viki Levitt, Anneliese Maus and Jake Tidmore, Warren Maus and Zim Loy, Robin McClellan, Laura Mielke, Martha Millard, Ben Pealer, Devin Rice, Jan Robbins, Wendy Rose, Cheryl Savageau, Siobhan Senier, Neal Surprenant, Lisa Tatonetti, Terry and Vivian Tiernan, Trudy and Michael Tritt, Eileen Visser, Carol Vossler, Kimberly Wieser, and Ruth Woodward.

For inquiries or to order additional copies, send correspondence to: Many Moons Press, 7 Cottage St., Potsdam, NY 13676 or e-mail derekmaus@gmail.com

ISBN-13: 978-0-692-11977-8

*For Stephanie and for Baby Oscar, who was born at almost the same time that this book was*

# TABLE OF CONTENTS

## Introduction
❖ Derek C. Maus

I never met Johnny Cash.

I've never been especially prone to being star-struck, so the fact that he was one of the few celebrities from my native Arkansas has very little to do with my regrets. I just love his music. I love it specifically for how it expresses both the lightness and the darkness within him so profoundly and forthrightly. I mean, come on…he wrote books entitled *The Man in Black* (his autobiography) and *The Man in White* (a novel about St. Paul). He was close friends with both the hell-raising Merle Haggard and the heaven-praising Billy Graham. He clearly knew a more than a little about living with the contradictory impulses that churn within every human. I don't share his religious faith, but I nevertheless recognized a kindred spirit in him as he gave artistic expression to both the angels and the demons of his nature. Alas, our paths never crossed before he left this world.

The happy ending to my part of this story is that I *did* meet somebody who walked a very similar line and sang about it in a voice that wasn't quite as deep as Johnny's sturdy bass-baritone, but nevertheless boomed with a comparable power and poignancy. Since you're holding this book in your hand, I suspect you know who I'm talking about…

I wish I had a little more inclination towards his brand of "poetic license" in telling tales, because if I did, I would surely stretch the truth a smidge and tell you that I met him for the first time as he walked into my office at SUNY Potsdam and said (in Cashian fashion)…

*Hello…I'm Maurice Kenny.*

Wouldn't that have been perfect? Yeah, well Maurice didn't steal his lines from anyone, so he surely wasn't going to rip off Johnny Cash for his opening. Actually, he sauntered in as I was unpacking boxes of books, took one look at the giant poster of John Coltrane's face that I had tacked up on the otherwise barren walls and said without any preamble whatsoever, "Hey! It's 'Trane! He and Alice used to live right around the corner from me back in Brooklyn."

Mind you, at this point I had absolutely no idea who this gregarious fellow with the white ponytail and the twinkling eyes might be, so the fact that he was claiming a personal relationship to yet another of my musical idols made me both curious and dubious at once. I certainly didn't anticipate that this was the start of a friendship that would gradually intensify over the course of fifteen years to the point that Maurice would somehow conclude that it would be a good idea for me to serve as the executor to his literary estate. I remain both honored and puzzled by his gesture of trust.

That first reactive flash of mixed emotions must surely have been a subconscious reckoning that I was in the presence of someone who shared with Johnny Cash the ability to evoke the full range of human feelings. As I began spending time with Maurice – and with his writing – I started to recognize that his was another voice capable of expressing lofty wonderment and joy alongside grim dread and imprecation.

The more I read his work, the more I noticed other shared tendencies. Both of them were famously cantankerous men who were not always the easiest people to put up with (I once digitally inserted Maurice's face into the infamous photograph of Johnny giving photographer Jim Marshall the middle finger from onstage and it ends up seeming completely plausible…try it for yourself if you don't believe me!). However, they each also possessed a sense of empathy that allowed them to imagine with equal facility the lovely and the loathsome, the lonely and the libertine.

Even though he apparently never spent more than a night or two in the drunk tank, Johnny was capable of singing from the perspective of a condemned prisoner on death row or that of a man so chillingly unemotional that he "shot a man in Reno/just to watch him die." In a wholly different context, Maurice mirrored this act of artistic self-projection by writing in the voice of the Jesuit missionary Isaac Jogues or that of William Johnson, two historical figures who played significant roles in the subjugation of the Iroquois. I feel as much regard for their portraits of these figures (towards whom each of them must have felt considerable personal contempt), as I do for Johnny's halcyon ditties about the simple pleasures to be found at "Cisco Clifton's Filling Station" or Maurice's tender evocations of Molly Brant or Frida Kahlo. The lesson I take from this is that one cannot simply turn away from ugliness, as much as one might want to. As another brilliant musician (and fellow Johnny Cash fan), Nick Cave, puts it in his song "Nature Boy," one must be "strong" and "bold" in the face of "ordinary slaughter" and "routine atrocity," because "in the end, it is beauty that is going to save the world."

Maurice understood that idealistic sentiment and embodied it throughout an artistic career that lasted more than six decades…and will hopefully outlive him for many more yet. The various pieces that are collected in this book are intended not simply as eloquent obituaries to his memory, but also as tributes to the transformative and inspirational effect that he had as a person, as an artist, as a friend, and as a teacher. Some of them were directly influenced by him and some of them are dedicated to him explicitly, while others were offered by their creators with the assurance that "I'm not quite sure what it is about this that reminds me of Maurice, but I can't escape the fact that it does so." They are all efforts to put a little more beauty in the world in response to the sense of loss that accompanied the news of Maurice's passing on April 16, 2016.

The title of the collection comes from a poem that Maurice wrote near the end of his life and which can be found immediately below. In it he makes clear his preference for the wild over the cultivated (a theme that pervades his work, particularly his well-known poem "Wild Strawberries"). Following his lead, we make here no pretense of being elegant hothouse specimens, but rather an unassuming cluster of spontaneous wildflowers to carry home. Scattered among our tributes you will also find more than two dozen of Maurice's own works here that have not previously been seen in print. These are intended as yet another sample of the soil from which these blossoms from his friends, students, and colleagues emerged. We hope you enjoy them all.

June 2018
Potsdam, NY

**June 28th, 2013**
❖ Maurice Kenny

*For Annie*

The waitress said, "I'll move the flowers…"
as if they bothered this group of diners.
It caught my ear as though she had made
a statement… consequently I stared.
It was a situation where two tables
were pushed together: the waitress
had brought the vase to it. She kind of smiled
in almost a curtsy and slammed the vase
down.

　　　They were bright daisies and
I had hoped from the road side growths;
not expensive ones from the flower shop.
It seemed real neat in such a fancy café
that would have sport to pick wild
daisies which probably spent centuries
growing for hands to carry them home
for stint at the dining table, or child's room.

But then in such an elegant café spelled
with an accent over the é…of course
they would be from their own green
garden or village botanical site…
　　　the wild ignored.

**Getting Old in the Adirondacks (A Practical Look)**
❖ Maurice Kenny

It's more than just the idea that pretty women don't smile at you any-more, or that college girls don't give a thought to whether their lusty youth catches your eye. They have no care, no interest. The desire is dead. Simple as that! It's not that companionship isn't out there, since it is in large numbers, although all under the age of 80 and over the age of 70. Not necessarily a turn-on in your eyes, when your eyesight is elsewhere, a spot nearer to 40 or 35.

This is to be expected, though not easily accepted or dealt with, when the wandering desire dissipates, hidden below the bed pillow, the smirk wiped off the lip, and the brain comes to the realization that there are far more important problems to face than a romantic relationship, should you be alone during the aging process. We can't all have a live-in nurse who tends to our every ache, a nurse who is sometimes known as a wife. Without a wife/nurse we'll roll up our sleeves and dig in im-mediately. Don't wait because those bones are rusty, out of practice and will stiffen immediately…. Exercise, loosen them up, as no nurse is on the way. Ask Dr. Oz.

If you are in a romantic situation, well, good luck, bon voyage, and swallow more vitamin B.

Should the brain not age as fast as the physical body, yea! That could be a problem. You want to shovel the first winter snow, put on your warm winter coat, get hat and gloves or wool mittens and head for the side-walk and driveway. The steps are covered by several inches; snow has actually spread to the front door of the veranda. You suck-in, breathe, heave a huge sigh and plow in with the shovel and instantly realize you have no breath for this foolish excursion into Mother Nature's de-bacle. Oh, but headstrong, macho to the heart attack, male to the end, you heft the shoulders, whistle a tune of "let it snow, let it snow," and commence to push, shove, and toss. Forty-five minutes later you have finished the short walk to the drive and the drive itself is clean…for the time being. Realizing the snow will continue falling, you scamper into the house, rub the cold from your hands and look for the Yellow Pages to find a young man to plow that miserable driveway. Your fellow cat looks at you with a most bizarre stare.

Age has set in. You can't breathe. It takes five to seven minutes to calm the lungs which give enough strength to take off your coat and boots. Oh yes, that's another sweet job: taking off the boots. Groans are evident; a near fall with the left boot; a curse that you will never wear them again, but then you discover the wet wool socks. Obviously, the boots leak. This time you sit down on a kitchen chair to pull the socks off, and being wet and having minds of their own, they won't budge from the heel. And there you go cursing again. Damn, damn! Suddenly you are confronted with a vision, a story from childhood:

My father had decided that he was to start me on the road to becoming a man. I was seven years old. He decided I needed to know the value of work and the sweat of money. He also knew that an older cousin, twelve years of age, was shoveling snow and earning dollars, having brought them home, strutting that he was a man. Morris was a husky lad for his age, well fed on gruel and salt pork. I was thin and suppered on the usual mac an' cheese, hamburgers, boiled potatoes, chicken soups, Spanish rice which was really not Spanish, or game when my father brought it home from the woods, tomatoes, onions, peppers and whatever herbs and spices my mother might have in the kitchen. She served these with her homemade bread, and if we were lucky, perhaps a monkey-dish of maple syrup for a sweet after. In no way was I starving, but our table diet was obviously different from that of Morris's mother's table fare. Whatever, my father was impressed with what he had made shoveling and could see no reason why I should not be out there on the sidewalks earning not just my keep, but a few pennies to boot.

My mother screamed, begged, threatened. He must not cause such a stupid, dangerous action. She pleaded I was a thin and sickly child. I'd die of pneumonia out there, be swept away by a blizzard, captured by gypsies – that trick sometimes worked. But he would not relent. He insisted that tomorrow morning she was to give me a solid hot breakfast, bundle me tightly, put a small shovel in my mittened hands and send me to the streets. She had to comply. He was boss, and I believe she feared his wrath. We were all well acquainted with it.

Within the hour, I was abducted and squired home by a city policeman who knew I was my father's child. With a wink he told my mother if he saw me again out there trying to find work by shoveling the business district walks, well, then he would arrest my father, and her. It was against the law for a child my age to work without a permit. And with a wink: "He trying to kill the kid?"

That ended that fiasco, though I was in bed several days with a heavy coughing cold and freezing feet. I believe he decided my manhood could wait a few years to begin.

The world is not a strange place, but those who inhabit the lands are certainly not always sensible. I loathed snow most of my life and to this minute reluctantly pick up a shovel to clean the porch or sidewalk. Shoveling is not one of the joys of the aged. I personally would rather watch the plow have the joy of heaving it into piles where you might play "king of the hill." I hated that game. I hated snow. I could not wait to get out of the North Country snow.

Shoveling snow is only one of the many tortures waiting. Again, just hoisting on boots or taking them off is sometimes as painful as putting on the winter coat. Just attempting to get the right arm and the left into the coat calls for much cursing; then zipping up the zipper that does not want to connect.

Oh, aging is lovely.

We are told that to be alone in your big house or small apartment is considered depressing. It isn't as such…not today with radio, TV, computers, time to watch birds fly in and build a new nest for their soon-to-be-born young. There is time, time for the doctor, the dentist, the surgeon, for high school lads to say no to "mowing your grass for a fiver," since they all have either ATM or charge cards. There is time to contemplate death, to be fitted for a coffin, checking that the name on the tombstone is spelled correctly. Always time to send Christmas cards with checks enclosed, much time to pet the cat or stroll with the dog, or chase kids from picking the lilacs and tossing them into the road; feeding chickadees, shouting at the grey squirrels or flailing hands at a buck/doe who wandered down off the mountain into the front yard to feast on your forsythia now seven years old but shorter than when you received it from a friend for a birthday. Blast the deer. Blast the red mosquitoes, the horrendous blackflies, the neighbor's sweet-smelling dryer fluids at eleven p.m. Blast all the new heavy traffic on your side road as many new condos shoot up in the woods two miles down the drive. Blast the old friends who have forgotten you because you're a bachelor and have no date with whom to attend the dinner parties. Blast the fact that you do not drive and do depend upon Tennessee Williams's "kindness of strangers" to get to the drug store or supermarket, or the doctor's office.

Aging is fun.

It is not the pain in the right leg upon settling down in bed for the night; it is not just the failing of sight, smell, or hearing, the weakness of the arm. It is not just that you are always cold and shouldn't turn up the heat to 70 but try to live with the thermostat at 62. It is not just because you cannot vacation for a month in Baja anymore or take a steam ship to Sicily. It is not because you can't climb Whiteface Mountain, paddle your canoe, beat up the local bully, read for more than half an hour before nodding off in the chair and slipping into a deep sleep. My mother did this and so will I.

Most people of an age are greatly worried about loss of memory. Not I. If I don't know why I went to the refrigerator it will pop up again later. I never thought I would need to stoop to the tactic of taking with me a photo of what I wanted, but it's true: many words escape; many names of former friends live in darkness; many treasures have disappeared… like the twenty-dollar bills I placed in many books for silly reasons, mainly *Candide*. Already signs have been tacked to the front door and the bedroom door asking, *did you remember to shut the oven off?* Memory is of the utmost importance, but the since mind is a computer that can hold only so much data, some of it must be deleted to make room for new facts and figures.

Aging is golden!

Bull turds. It's a pain in the royal wazoo. There is no fun, little joy, almost no sense of accomplishment unless it is a successful bowel movement, or you're able to tie your shoelaces, or remember not to fall asleep in the bathtub and awake only when the water is frigid. That is a rare sense of accomplishment.

Too grow old is delightful.

With ache and pain, loss of sight, with fears of falling, tripping, with less money in the bank account as there has been no work and possibly no savings or retirement plan, having worked forty years as an office clerk or such; living barely, on social security, which is not rich life; definitely no vacations except on the front porch rocking your time away with fading memories and an old cat unable to control its bladder while napping on your lap; knowing you should paint the veranda rockers and tables; you should plant tulips the next spring, climb up and pour seed into the birds' feeder; to remember the sweet water for the hummingbirds' bowl; not to forget to call Aunt Agnes, who has just turned 94 – and to remember to pay the phone bill.

We keep saying over and over as we stand in front of the bathroom mirror or the full-length bedroom mirror that it is not the aches or the loss of quickness, that a foxtrot is absolutely out of the question, that eating a bowl of maple walnut ice cream before bed is out; or that pizza is forgotten; that reflux stymies most delicious foods such Thai or Mexican. It is not these wonders and delights and favorites. It is that life is passing you by. Your fingers are not in its dirt anymore. You contribute nothing. You are not up for the salary increase or promotion but for the "meals on wheels" lady to visit and bring a touch of living to you. *Oh, how is the world out there?* you ask. She smiles as if to say there is nothing there for you but this plastic container of bad cooking. That is the world. And you wonder if the food came from China...cooked or raw. And you ask, *Are you going to Wal-Mart perchance?* with the hope that she might take you there as though it were a zoo from childhood, or a movie from youth. Again the smile and it says, *Not for you, grandpa, not for you. Not today and possibly not forever.* And her smile walks off the porch and you are left with the tin of cooling food in your lap: a thin slice of very tough beef which you don't eat, mashed potatoes without butter or gravy, one slice of oleoed bread, and sodden green string beans. Oh well, you don't have teeth anyway.

You want to bury your head in the pillow and cry. Not because you can't chew a rare steak or climb to the tenth floor of the tallest building in the town, or because smiles are deceiving and hold the knowledge that you are old, old, withered, wrinkled, that you mumble, that drool slips from your mouth onto a vest which is in dire need of washing, that you hold a tainted smell of urine, that your right hand shakes and you need help to rise from the rocking chair, that someone should make your bed which hasn't been changed for two-and-a-half weeks, that mice haunt the kitchen because your cat is too old to hunt and kill, that the house reeks of old cooked food, that a cleaning person once had the kitchen spotless and now it's a near ruin in the sense that the dirt on the floor is inching, the grease on the stove is – oh well. All that is to be expected from the "meals on wheels" lady's smile as she slowly backs away and down the steps, terrified that it will rub off on her one day, perhaps sooner than later, as she is no spring chicken herself.

You want to cry.

Go ahead, cry. Let the tears fall, beat the cold pillow but don't kick the cat: it's not the cat's fault that your hand shakes, or that you cannot see the TV screen clearly, that you left the oven on. You can't afford the furnace to run hotter than 62, so you pull a blanket about your shoulders and wait for the warmth of spring, the hot summer sun, the balmy nights of autumn…and then, then you might be dead and won't have to worry about the cold, or that the mortuaries are getting richer on your old skin, your tired blood, your cold feet, the empty bank account, your fear and the anger that lives with that fear. *Oh, it is awesome*, as the kids might say. *Awesome!*

Once dad or mom or both protected you, then a teacher, a spouse, a daughter or a son, and now – aren't you lucky? – you have the AARP to sell you insurance you can't afford, to buy your medicines which you can't afford and to speak to the government for you since you can't speak. Hurrah for that company which gives succor to your aging bones, your wrinkling skin, your disappearing vision! Better than Social Security or Medicare. Nothing to say…out of fear that someone might read this sometime, who probably delights in watching your savings slowly disappear to the fuel companies, the telephone, the cable monopolies, especially to China for their onions, to South Africa for their navel oranges, Indonesia for its pollution, and these United States of America, for its wars against other humans, for its lack of care about the world in general unless it possesses oil for the bad cars we produce and which wreck the atmosphere. But then again, the old are alleged to be bitter, paranoid, disgruntled in general, disappointed, failures and deservedly so, and who consequently blame it all on the government and the young for causing so many problems in the world. The aged are guilty. Sever their heads, cut out their tongues. You can't make them happy until…

…until God…

who/whatever god is or God may be calls them home. Home? Where is home? In the dirt, the mud, the soil, the land of birth, a cemented crib, a metal container if you're wealthy enough, or a pine box if you're dirt poor. Who cares anyway…the dead? The living? Only those not in the will, or only those there to pay the bills left behind, especially the fuel bill. Where is Eliot Spitzer when you need him? I'll take Cuomo if there is no one else.

Bitch, bitch, bitch. The joy of the aged, the pleasure, the only use they are good for. I mean, what we're only good for is to bitch and complain.

The golden years. As I said – bull.

It is not the ache in the arm or leg or little toe. It is not the loss of vision or hearing or a woman in bed, a warm smile, the touch of a furry kitten. It is not the wrinkles about the eyes, the hair in your ears, the groan when eliminating or bending to pick up a pin, or burning a finger when you light a match, or choke on an apple, or when your penis leaks in bed at night which embarrasses you profoundly.

It can only be thought that the world is passing and you are not passing with it, that this is an important part of the passing no matter how un-important the part is…a simple human being with passion and possibly love and possible respect and an eye which sees, a hand which touches, a face that feels the autumn breeze and smells the spring on the lilacs flung into the road by young boys who tore a branch from the bush.

The dark will be enough. To rest forever without worry, without cold, without need, and never know loneliness, the hunger of the soul, the spirit. To be content at last to sleep, a dreamless sleep, never cold, never warm, never wanting…anything, neither a kiss nor a plum.

But is it truly darkness, emptiness, nothingness? Or was life nothing-ness, useless, wasteful? As my body rots, as maggots feed into the empty flesh, as dust becomes me, my thoughts will live, live without the pain of age, the toothless grin or hair in the ears. Thoughts I had sent out into whatever air, to live in whatever ear, though those people hearing may not breathe as I once breathed, though in time not a single ear may recognize from where those thoughts came, as if from the void – or possible void – they will live and grow where thoughts may go into what wonder, imagination, process.

And aging then will not matter…the ache caused by whatever means, or breeze of breath, or slap on the cheek. Life will have become useful, ripe with meaning.

We do not pain nor perish but live within another's mind.


**Wild**
❖ Maurice Kenny

A foot could not help
Stepping on the leaf
Not only tiny but
Insignificant to the foot
Which cannot see.

Off in shadows blackbirds
Eye those white buds about
To whisper in a small voice:
I'm feeling strength move,
And shortly I'll show the world
What a tiny thing like me can be.

Two grey squirrels wait not so
Patiently for a sweet treat of
Red pulp. They sit on low
Branches of an ash waiting their
Time knowing treats would
Soon be theirs if the foot
Took more careful steps,
Or if the children of the house
Did not squeal and get there first.
Neither knew this very wild
Strawberry, the first fruit
Of spring brings new life.

**time travel one**
❖ Randy Lewis

Apple blossoms in full bloom
undaunted by wild spring wind,
bounce on heavy branches
full of promise –
bees with all their empty buzzing
nuzzle in sweet white flowers
blow away,
come back again

Fragrant pale blossoms
only last a little while,
tumble in warm twisting gusts,
fall into mad raging rivers,
pile on brown muddy ground,
white confetti spent, after the great parade.

May offers an uneasy gift
of seeing time ahead of time.
When small green buds begin to form
on the ends of empty branches,
sometimes I see blossoms instead.
When bees come to flowers, drunk and dancing,
I blink and suddenly
the cold wet earth washes white with petals,

and when tiny green apples come to twiggy limbs,
cheerful nubby balls holding on
for their fattening trip through summer,
I see November's branches, dark,
empty
save for one last unpicked apple, gold and round
and all around me
falls the snow

**3 Days Before My Birthday**
❖ Maurice Kenny

Blinded by a nagging pain
I stood rain pouring all
around and as a winding sheet
folding I turned west then east
and knew not which turn to take

I felt like Kerouac, his few days
left in the rainbows of life, crushed
into a West Village doorway looking
for Paradise in the New York Blues.

There I was with winding roads
far behind and only a cloud or something
like a cloud before/over a path into stars
where nothing reached for my hand.
Unlike Jack no editor waited my image
to tack to any wall open and free.

Tony, my heart man, not far, and breathing
deep I sought an executor for my soul, soul
without color or tissue. And again like Jack
in the dark doorway, my head bent and could not
lead me to the sun shining in the movie
playing down the street, a musical: "West Side
Story" and I was caught between the Jets
and Sharks, and like Jack no young
Puerto Rican miss smiling into my heart.

On feet moving the classic molasses
my damn clock continued to move
and helped push me to Tony who would
take my heart, rub it in his medical hands,
take some blood, check oxygen and send
me back to streets, return to fears of a sleep
so long no clock could count those hours
spent with fingers crossed but teeth chattering.

Surely it was that road taken, yes, that road
and I would not need to walk far to its
blackened end, the doorway
that I could share with Kerouac.

**waterfalls**
❖ Randy Lewis

every time
the lay of the land changes
the river roars
in excitement and terror
spilling over
from one world to the next
foaming and babbling
to tell you
how to be free

you do not turn around,
you can't –
you spill over and over,
only getting larger, better
only becoming the sea
you were meant to be
following this very route
since the beginning
of time

**raise your right hand**
❖ Randy Lewis

**Do you solemnly swear**
(sometimes, but not as much as I used to,
does saying "damn" count?)
**to tell the truth**
(of course, of course
I am an honest person –
always have been, always hope to be)
**the whole truth**
(every single bit?
Even what I don't remember?
Even the smell of the summer air,
the names of people I have harmed
by thoughtlessness
and someone who once made me cry?)
**and nothing but the truth**
(no part of everyday chatter?
No part of mindless gossip?
Nothing like "how do you do?"
or "nice day, isn't it?"
when you don't care one bit
and saying nothing at all
fills the spaces so loudly
that your knees cave in
and your temperature rises?)
**so help you God?**
(so help *me*, God?
Whose God are we speaking of?
My god is not here
in this courtroom –
My god is a good god, a kind god
and lives in the forest, high
in the trees, and fast in the brook, not
here among the dark wooden benches
and conniving, thieving lawyers
who make an awful lot of money,
prefer to be called attorneys,
speak an invented language,

look through people instead of at them,
and leap and lunge at every small piece
of truth that has a catch to it,
a manmade catch to it
which makes guilt out of air
and innocence a crime –
where is there a god here?
And *helping* me? Please,
who exactly did you say
is helping me?)
**I do.**
**You may be seated.**

## A Few Words on An Old Friend and Fellow Author
❖ Duane Niatum

Maurice Kenny and I first met in the early 1970s when I was the editor
of Harper & Row's Native American Authors Program. We started a
long telephone and letter exchange when I began gathering poems for
the first anthology, *Carriers of the Dream Wheel*, which was published
in 1975. Maurice did not appear in this first collection only because the
press kept me to a small gathering of sixteen poets, no more.

I spent about three years convincing Harper & Row to allow me to edit
a second, larger volume of American Indian poetry. Maurice was one of
the new poets that would enrich the scope of the earlier collection, and
add an impressive dimension to the range and quality of the volume.
His work and the work of other poets showed readers and the public a
new generation and the spirit of an age-old people of song and story.
The work made clear, without a uniformity of subject matter, metaphor,

or style, that American Indian poets were carrying with them a common cultural heritage, expressed in divergent and often stunning ways. They gladly offered a voice that will not die. In fact, it has grown and is growing from a body that speaks of blood and flesh and passion and dream rooted in the earth, water, and air of their ancestors who nourish the words they write and ground those words in the moment. Maurice illustrates this perfectly in his poem "Legacy":

> My face is grass
> > Color of April rain;
> Arms, legs are the limbs
> > Of birch, cedar;
> My thoughts are winds
> > Which blow;

The things of this world spoke to this poet who transformed them into images and symbols. His verse solidly joins the land to the inner man. He knew where his journey would take him by looking and listening closely to how the world lives in its particulars around him. As Theodore Roethke once said, "I learn by going where I have to go."

For every poet worth his lines, the earth teaches him the path to take on his journey of discovery and renewal. Maurice recognized this from the beginning and never wavered in his forming of the wordsmith's path. This character he displayed is why we became lifelong friends and why I grieved for a long time after he died. Now that I am at the winter grounds of my life, it seems clear as mountain water that Maurice was one of my oldest and dearest friends. I managed to come around and heal because poets like Maurice are still with us in the poems and stories they share with us. His poet's staff will withstand any wind that comes its way even though we recognize that poets are forgotten almost before they die.  It is the American tradition!

Seattle, WA
November 2017

**for Maurice Kenny, his way of resistance**
❖ Béatrice Machet

shadowy as it seems                           as small as it appears
an area in your mind                    like a little shrug
*something that will end up in shivers*
then a growling storm rising and you'll hear

be**tray**al betrayal **betrayal**

you've been fooled and you lay lost in the dark
looking up for some moonlight      for a star to glow
shadowy as it seems
your hands held up
to read the facts and know
if cruelty prevails    beware
awake and don't miss your **vision** the dream
you are in other's rolling eyes the dice
they'll steal to break your line
an area in your heart they'll trample upon
and stomping they'll lean at ease on your rebounding skill
the absurdity of killing each other is      not dead

shadowy as it seems the scar
what's sacred
has been laughed at                  if not violated
but your voice
shadowy as it seems:

                   *subpoena me and I'll suppoema you*
                   *hand in a glove*
                   *I'll be your sleeping dragon*
                   *suing you*

**Naughty, Probably**
❖ Maurice Kenny

I loved always
                    plums
round and purple
touched lightly by morning dew
cold to tongue's first lick

I could never wait for
                    jam
on breakfast toast
sweet to lips, tongue
as juice runs down the
                            throat

I have loved always
                    plums
significant to boyhood
as manhood rises to claim
hair growing on the chin
as soon whiskers tickle

Plums do not last long
they hang a day
                    and
then wither overnight
until not even a wild child
will push away the dark
to steal a
                    bite

I have always loved
                    plums

**A Bloom of Native American Poetry**
❖ Stephen Lewandowski

To get flowers (or poems) to bloom someone has to till the earth, plant and fertilize the seed, and fight off the weeds.

The Benedictine Blue Cloud Abbey was established in 1955 primarily to serve residents of the nearby Lakota (Sioux) Reservations. It appears that the advent of Brother Benet (Denis) Tvedten, OSB at the Benedictine Blue Cloud Abbey in Marvin, South Dakota began a new chapter in the history of first upper Midwestern poetry and later Native American poetry on the national level. It appears that the first *Blue Cloud Quarterly* that was edited by Brother Tvedten was published in 1971, though I only learned of *BCQ* in the mid-70s while living in Minneapolis. The first issue I saw – volume XXI, number 4 – included Maurice Kenny's "Indian Burial Grounds – Northern New York" and "Corn Planter."

*Blue Cloud Quarterly* began as a magazine featuring the work of six to eight Native American poets per issue. But as time went by, and contacts with the writing community strengthened, *BCQ* increasingly became a series of chapbooks by some well-known, some obscure, some to-be-better-known Native American poets. To name a few: Wendy Rose, Karoniatatie, Norman Russell, Ralph Salisbury, Adrian Louis, Mary Tall Mountain, Joseph Bruchac, William Oandasan, Elizabeth Cook-Lynn, Duane Niatum, Lance Henson, and Paula Gunn Allen.

Maurice and the *Blue Cloud Quarterly* were both deeply implicated in the growing interest in Native American poetry during the 1970s. The success of such books as Jerome Rothenberg's *Shaking the Pumpkin*, Geary Hobson's *The Remembered Earth*, and Duane Niatum's *Carriers of the Dream Wheel* testified to an opening that had not previously existed and both Maurice and *BCQ* stepped through that door. The chapbooks of Maurice's poetry that *Blue Cloud Quarterly* published include several of his most highly regarded works, such as *Dancing Back Strong the Nation* (1979), *North: Poems of Home* (1979), and *The Smell of Slaughter* (1982). He was the single poet most published by the *Blue Cloud Quarterly* during the last half of the 1970s. They also published two works that would be later reprinted by White Pine Press: *Wounds Beneath the Flesh* (1983), an anthology of fifteen Native American poets, and the short-story collection *Rain and Other Fictions* (1985).

The tenth anniversary issue of 1981 is dedicated to "Maurice Kenny, poet, publisher, editor and supportive friend" by Brother Benet. Maurice has three poems, "Tonight We Go to Hear Muriel Rukeyser Read Her Poems at SUNY Buffalo, 1978 (Now, In Memory)," "Gone Fishing," and "Canyon de Chelly." By 1981, Maurice was encouraging and publishing other Native American poets through his Strawberry Press and serving a wider literary audience by co-editing *Contact/II* in New York City.

It's hard to remember how parochial the canon of poetry was in 1970. No women to speak of, hardly any openly gay and lesbian writers, no Native Americans, no notion of the poetry and poetics of the rest of the world. Dead white men. *Blue Cloud Quarterly* and Maurice Kenny were pioneers in connecting writers, in creating a place where Native Americans could speak to one another, while expanding the whole notion of poetry. My hat's off to *Alcheringa*, *Technicians of the Sacred*, *Come to Power*, to *Akwesasne Notes*, *South Dakota Review*, and the *Greenfield Review* for bringing new words to the blissfully unaware American poetry community. I know…I was one, I was there, asleep.

**Author's Note:** Those seeking more information about this time and these people are advised to consult Bethany Ann Yardy's thesis from the University of Texas at Arlington, *A Labor of Love: A Social and Literary History of the Blue Cloud Quarterly* (2014).

## The Frailties of Consequence
❖ Derek C. Maus

Outcomes and expectations –
   the setup precedes the knockdown
upon consideration of the backwards chain
trailing from the misunderstood nowness.

What is desired to stand for truth
    only serves to fill the spaces
where links – severed, ignored, or otherwise gapped –
have gone asunder, and no explanation comes forth.

To know is not simply to perceive
    and to perceive is not simply to think;
Transitively, the lesson is a simple one,
were it so that practice is a matter of arithmetic zeal.

The mantras and proverbs of insight
    hold no power in the face of will,
bent to the maintenance of high towers,
shielding the what-should-be from the what-is.

**Snow, Snow Snow (an excerpt from *A Step Too Far*)**
❖ Maurice Kenny


A flake falls to an eyelash
                              then
lights on a tongue
                              then
a breeze of snow
                              drops
into an empty valley
                              and
a wind of snow rushes
                              turns
landscape into a different
                              land,
known world is in a whirl

a blizzard whirling circles
                              and
circles whirling this world
                              out
of human sight; not a footprint
to be found, or echo on winds'
bluster yet feet walk, trudge
                              over snow
struggle, fall, misstep, face
                              drops
against freezing, falling
                              flake
married to cheek


whirls and whirls cover land

and sky darkens to the insistence
                              of
day and time and a long night
                              to
follow… …. …

wind sweeps across
                          breath
of both beast and man


Harsh, a harsh land
nor cruel, not mean
except in spring when
blackflies are in damp
woods and bite

——————————


harsh, a harsh land
it can be, but not mean

mountains tough to climb
hills hard to cultivate
valleys much too far
to hike; rivers deep, wide
forests; then snows or rains
or summer heat, winter's
long cold mornings

a hard land, harsh
it can be, but not mean

take years to level
fields of those mighty trees

————————————————


wolf prints, bear, beaver
wild cat, rabbit, skunk
cougar, fox paws…
red and silver
snake, moose, elk, white tails
beaver, beaver, more beaver
and more boot prints
soft moccasin prints
alone deep in winter snow
spring mud, ever so deep
in oozing mud prints

of heel and toe… heel and toe
mink, grouse, woodcock
then beaver begins to decline
in numbers – wiped out
fewer teeth marks on a birch limb
fewer castles in ponds,
but more boot prints in snow

_____
_____

harsh, very harsh … mean, cruel
sun began to set
on dirtied snow
covering beaver bones
wolf tracks, cougars

**So Unlike the Death It Resembles**
❖ Derek C. Maus


Footsteps echo down the hallway still
long beyond the time when shoes trod
whether lightly, as in sneaking or consideration,
or heavily, as in drunken stumble or upset.

Dust has nestled on clothes abandoned,
books never-gotten-to,
forlorn objects stripped of their care,
    but not of their signification.

Walls unadorned now, where pictures hung
radiate their colors too vividly.
The bed, wide as a river and half-warm,
fills the room inadequately and excessively at once.

Scraps of words, sentences in a hand no longer refreshed
clutter the cabinets, drawers and surfaces.
Even smells linger like punished children,
lurking in corners until freed again to play.

This is not death, though resemblance in the mind
is hard to avoid when sifting through remnants
of life undone, plans unmade.
Steps in sequence hereafter feel unsafe and unsure.

**Not of the Living**
❖ Maurice Kenny

no bird flies
no leaf falls
nor is river heard
dashing to sea

seems no sun rises
no wave touches shore
no mosquito bites
no bee gathers honey

no moon warms
a cold pillow
no dream rises
in the middle of the night

no toe touches
under quilts of bed
no cat purrs
nor dog barks to go out

no one knocks
on a closed door
to see if anyone
needs a tiny smile

**A Red Rose**
❖ Oscar Sarmiento

*For Jonell McCray*

A red rose,
not
a carnation,
I will bring to you.
A rose,
though I am
no gardener.
Yes,
for your life
and
your silence,
your persistent smile,
a rose
like nothing much.
The rose
your mom could have given
to you,
your dad.
It takes, sometimes,
a stranger
to think of a rose,
the same stranger who,
you see,
pulls it out of his hat.
A rose
should be,
I feel, a promise,
nothing
to brag about.
Petals,
thorns,
aroma,
strong enough to awaken
moon dust,
to bring back

more,
many more,
yes,
roses in bloom.
The stranger,
the lunatic if you will,
will come up to you
a rose on his open palm,
entrusting you
forever,
this second,
to grant the flower
its shine,
its shadow,
its silhouette,
more than a ghost,
more than a spirit,
more than his own breath,
surviving only for you,
for your smile,
for your sweet
salute to the windy day,
for your silence
and the vibrant aroma
of your heart
rooted, yes,
deeply rooted
in all your own
days and days to come.
Keep, please,
this in mind,
a red rose
ready to glow for nothing
on a stranger's
open palm.

### The Spring's First
❖ Maurice Kenny

Wild
      wild
first tiny blooms
        as though singing
        in morning sun
        as it clutches earth

what pleasure
        to waken to
        cherries
wild and green this
           moment
        but June will be
        a different song
           they will burst
           red, red…strawberry red
though robins, bluejays, and finches
will pluck them all
before any boy's tooth
will break their sweet skin

we though shall sink teeth
into sweet burgundy flesh
riding trains across
Germany

**indian time misunderstood**
❖ gabor g gyukics


when the Watersprinkler is playing his flute
on a 21$^{st}$ century tenement corner
where the sun heats up the brick
to the rhythmical sound of ripe pears
falling through the branches reach the ground
end up erupting inside your greedy fingers

bouncing on and off pretending
to be otherworldly plants
in front of an underwater gaudí backdrop
there, then and anywhere, anytime
consider and muse on the prospects of names
that might be nothing else

but references words when people are not present
for correlation not equaling causation in any
of the mitigated incongruities in the vanishing spring
while every other day
thousands of mantis deflorate billions of
buffalo grass, grama, sage, chamiza, snakeweed

so now it's time
to bade your copacetic moments of erectile sequences
and outrig the currently provided diaphanous life sentence
in every pond surrounded by fields lay in beds of red poppies
to tie the conglobated matter into something
that belongs only to your disguised self

among bunches of stinging nettles trying
to perform cunnilingus on an unevenly balanced
botanically active female meat-eater
who wants to turn you over
and gobble you after you finish
getting rid of your camouflage

wondering how will you end up
thinking of nothing in particular

looking at a wounded mirror whose host
never again will call anyone out on their names
to avoid falling out of its ready made
amalgamated framework of ground glass

greedy fingers consider and muse on
every reference word surrounded by fields
of stinging nettles hurting nothing in particular

### When Talking with Rimbaud
❖ Maurice Kenny

I can't believe in color
                               s
I can't believe in line
                               s
there's a mistake
                      no one can
colors are traitors
lines shall hang around the neck
                                    tight
pulling even tighter
                         until…

colors were glorious when a child:
the lollypop, the cotton candy,
the very thought of pistachio
                              green
green how will we have our garden green
green songs, green hair, a green tongue
a green thumb, an elm, a hair braid,
curls on christmas boughs

I can't believe in colors
they make nightmares
                         when children
                                     scream

**Deer Poem**
❖ Marty Thompson

Grass leaders,
I have killed the buck
whose fawns will devour me.

For three seasons
I have watched
the six point buck
drink my spring water, eat my summering grass and fall sweet corn;
dancing down sunstreaks
he came
in early winter.
I shot him.

      He moves,
      and is not lost.

I pull the steaming paunch
from his frame,
and know the traditional
first kill meal of liver
and garden onions.

      When I die
      and move to the earth,
      my bones will sprout more summer grass.

## The Elk
❖ Neal Burdick

*NEWS ITEM: In the 1930s, authorities at the Debar Game Management Area in the northern Adirondacks received as a gift several elk from the American West, and began an attempt to establish a breeding population in the region. The first pairs to be released were quickly shot by hunters, who claimed they thought they were deer. Others escaped through breeches in their enclosure, caused either by poachers or by their own antlers, and were never seen again. Wildlife experts believe the last one died sometime in the 1950s.*

Under white cedars on a low rise, the elk bellowed across the marsh, the frozen surface streaked by sleet and snow, the hardwood slope beyond obscured, gaunt black spruces in the marsh bent before the wind.

There was no reply.

His antlers were heavy, heavier than he'd ever known them to be. Nor had he known it be so cold.

He lowered his head, folded his legs beneath him and drifted into sleep. He'd passed many nights in this place, enveloped in the delicate yellow-greens of spring, the sullenness of summer, the knife edge of autumn, the grey and white of winter as one season melted into another and another. He'd fed on the marsh's hearty dripping vegetation in warm weather, browsed on sprigs of cedar in cold. He'd known the marsh when it was redolent of rain, when it was pierced by cold, when it nourished him and when it starved him.

He'd left the marsh often. He'd wandered and wandered again the northern Adirondacks, in search of his own kind. He'd seen bears and coyotes, moose and deerflies, otter and eagle. Where once long trains had frightened him off, he'd followed abandoned railroad beds, sandy and straight, ducking into the forest on the rare occasions when a vehicle appeared. He'd paused at empty hunters' shacks, sniffed the air, pawed the garbage dumps, marked the strawberry patches. He'd forded rivers, clambered up ridges of maple and beech, prowled bogs and mires. Rocks, waters and alders had been his companions. He'd traveled in the dawn and the dusk, the galaxies on the edges of their visible lives, resting in the center of each day and through the nights, however long those nights lasted in the frigid times. Patience was his greatest strength.

He'd avoided the highways with their noises and their speed and the carcasses of animals not as wise as he. And he'd avoided the towns and the upland farms on the fringes of the great forest. His was a wilderness world, a world of continual movement, of silence, of solitude.

Only twice in all these times had he seen a human. Once, in a clearing, a man in a wool plaid jacket had raised a rifle toward him. He'd turned and plunged into thicker woods, his brown coat blending with the mosaics of the land, the gun's report reverberating across the swamps and far-off hardwood hills until it faded away. Years later, after he'd found himself on the edge of a picnic ground, someone had raised a thin black object in both hands, tapped it, lowered it and stared until he'd turned away to blend once more. There had been no reverberation.

He'd returned often to the wetlands, for here was food, drink, memory. Here was hope. Past and future merged into timelessness beyond the boundaries of time, and he was home. And it did not change. Snow slashed and sun burned and thunder echoed off unseen cliffs and leaves fell, and it did not change.

Under white cedars on a low rise the elk awoke. Slowly he raised his head and bellowed across the marsh.

(photo taken about a quarter-mile from Maurice's apartment on April 16, 2016)

**Rendezvous, a Vision of My Father**
❖ Marty Thompson

You stand cradling a rifle,
lever action, and looking west,
clad in green and black jacket,
gray pants, colors of hemlock and beech

next to the stick cabin
on the low ridge above Skinner Creek
where we are to meet in the last
dim light of day.

I see you crouch wraith-like
and sight along the barrel
at some distant deer crossing water –

and your eye, the front blade
and his shoulder line up.  Your
finger tickles the trigger and
the buck bolts and is gone.

Muddy water eddies in heart shapes
at creek's edge, tendrils of crimson
point through second growth so thick
a man cannot walk there, yet

the deer is in there, and will die
as certainly as you, and as soon.
my eye holds you, deer, stream, greenbrier
in the darking. And you do not know
I have seen you shoot; you light
a smoke, hands shaking, and sit, back to hemlock and me and pray
your aim was true.

## Dove Hunting
❖ Colin Pope

*for Maurice Kenny*

If you have to kill a symbol it's best
to do it alone,

tiptoeing between downed branches,
vigilant to the limb-crotches of evergreens
for a poorly constructed nest.
You'll strain just to notice them as birds,

having overlooked their plainness
as a nuisance of gray and brown
your entire life, and yet more difficult to see

their wingtips with your ears
when they cut the hallways of the forest
to that inborn whistling, like a sound
from a broken wheel. Someone

had to notice them first; it's become
almost easier to believe the trees themselves
are chirring in mourning.
Picture a starving man, scanning

for the trills of false pain in a wood,
paused until the air
closes around a precise tunnel

which slows such blurs for a knockdown.
You have to turn yourself off

to witness all this perception, its million eyes,
to know exactly which kind of peace
you must destroy to survive.

### Driving Mister Maurice
❖ Ed Kanze

There were multiple ways to know Maurice Kenny. One could attend a poetry reading and marvel at the way this man of modest stature (which is to say, he wasn't tall) could assume enormous proportions in front of an audience and hold every listener in the palm of his hand. One might take a writing class with him and feel both the nurture of his lionhearted encouragement and the terrible swift sword of his unsheathed criticism. One might meet him at a dinner party or be introduced to him in a restaurant or coffee shop and be doubtful of the gentle shake of his soft hand or, as he dropped the names of universities where he'd taught and the American Book Award he'd won and the European venues that were begging him for further poetry readings, the seeming oversized dimensions of his ego. But I venture to say the best way to know Maurice, and the means by which a great many of his friends got to know and love him better than they otherwise might, may well have been to drive him somewhere.

He was always cadging rides. Apparently he wasn't especially particular about who chauffeured him because he first pressed me into service as one of his drivers at a time when we hardly knew each other. New friends drove Maurice, old friends, colleagues, and, in a pinch, someone who happened to stand nearby rattling car keys. I never asked Maurice why he habitually recruited drivers rather than driving himself. On the face of it, his passenger habit had everything to do with the fact that he didn't own a car. But surely there was more. Third-hand, I heard an explanation from a source I cannot attribute because I cannot remember who it was. The tale involved a tragedy involving an automobile in another country and a vow to never drive again. Maybe there's a grain – or a sand pile – of truth in the story. Maurice had driven cars in the past, he had the means to own a car, and yet in the midst of a culture and a geography in which it's almost impossible to live without a motor vehicle, he lived without one – well, if not actually without one, then without owning one or getting behind a wheel.

In an effort to stir up memories of time spent in cars with Maurice, I circulated a request for stories to a short list of his friends. Perhaps because I warned that I needed brief passages about a character who defies reduction, the responses were few. But in them came nuggets of gold.

Tim Fortune – who along with his wife, Diana, introduced Maurice to my wife, Debbie, and me – responded in a flash. His words came in the fond, bemused tone in which Tim always spoke of his longtime friend. "Most of what I did," Tim wrote, "was drive him from my studio to [his] home on occasion. He would never ask, just wait for me to inquire about his day, and it would inevitably lead to me asking if he needed a ride. He would sit in the bench outside my gallery and wait for me to bring the car around, sort of his 'bus stop.' I always marveled at him carrying a backpack and how much he walked everywhere."

While Tim got to know Maurice as a fellow creative artist, Caroline Hotaling began her acquaintance with him when she was a student in a class he was teaching at North Country Community College in Saranac Lake. "He was a great teacher," she recalls, "and my friends and I ended up at his house for dinner several times a week."

Caroline recalled two stand-out drives with Maurice. One involved her chauffeuring him from Saranac Lake to Long Island, near New York City. "Driving through the bridges and tolls around NYC he would talk a lot about [a past] lover," she recalls, "a woman who was Puerto Rican, and I think [was] named Rose. He [was] reminded by the bridges and tolls of places they had gone, her brother's concern for her, and how much he loved her."

But the most memorable road trip Caroline made with Maurice Kenny was a drive stretching out over many days from New York to Bisbee, Arizona. The year, she thinks, was 1996, about eleven years after they first met. "We stayed with many friends and visited historic [and] Native American sites along the way," she wrote.

Foremost in Caroline's memory of the Arizona expedition is the fact that she drove an old Nissan whose front passenger door was rusted shut. "At the age of sixty-seven," she wrote, "Maurice climbed in and out of the car window to get in the car. He liked to have me (a cute young thing at the time...) pull up to a high curb close to some onlookers, preferably older, so they could see him climb in my car window and speed off with [an attractive] young woman. This was one of our many daily amusements."

Derek Maus, a colleague of Maurice's at SUNY Potsdam, shared a story that gives us the poet as passenger at his quirky, quintessential best. Derek had driven to the airport in Syracuse to pick up Maurice, flying in from Europe via Rome. Maurice, then eighty-two, had done some traveling around the continent on his own after delivering a keynote address at a conference in Austria. Derek hadn't heard a word from his friend in ten days and was just starting to wonder if Maurice was going to turn up at all when he materialized in a hallway, a backpack hanging from one shoulder.

He shared a piquant account of their three-hour drive to Saranac Lake.

> Had I not known him for more than ten years at that point, I would have been tempted to presume he was making up some of the stories he was telling me.
>
> He told me about trying to find his connecting train in the Zurich train station while suffering from a 101-degree fever that he'd started feeling on the long ride from Vienna to Zurich.
>
> He told me about the three days of being nursed back to health by Béatrice Machet and her husband, in their chalet in the Genevan Alps.

He told me about the three days and nights he spent walking around Barcelona by himself (he never managed to get together with the old friend who invited him) eating seafood, drinking coffee, and jovially arguing with cranky waiters in the Mexican-accented Spanish he'd picked up nearly five decades earlier.

He told me about being briefly arrested by the *carabinieri* in Milan after being mistaken for a homeless Turkish immigrant while sleeping on a bench in the train station during his long layover there.

He told me about being befriended by a "Sophia Loren look-alike" (of course…) woman named Maria, who worked for Alitalia and helped him find a room in a seaside hotel outside Rome after his initial reservation somehow fell through. By the time he actually boarded his flight back to New York from Rome, Maria had passed him along to Christina, who apparently doted on him in his preferred manner all the way across the ocean, right down to moving him into one of the bulkhead seats that would give him less of a feeling of confinement.

My slight sense of horror that this meandering tale of adventure could have gone horribly wrong at about ten different moments was counterbalanced by my marvel at his unwavering ability to thread the needle of living by his wits and charm.

Derek's tale concluded as many of them do, "It felt like I had been listening to the pitch for a Fellini film, but I have nary a doubt that (nearly) every word of it was true."

My own memories of drives with Maurice are strangely vivid and vague at the same time. Vivid are the feelings of time, place, and mood, and vague are my recollections of the flood of colorful pronouncements, opinions, observations, advice, and commentary that poured from him every time we sat beside each other in a car. Derek mentioned that he wished he'd recorded Maurice during their drive home from Syracuse. I wish I'd done the same during our trips together. Sadly, I didn't even take notes. I keep a journal, but I think the fact that after an hour in Maurice's company my head was spinning in so many different directions explains why it lay beyond me, after the fact, to write coherent accounts.

I do remember that on my longest drive with him – which might also have been the last – he spoke at length, sometimes at great length, about people he esteemed and people he loathed. With Maurice there didn't seem to be much middle ground. I always hoped that because Maurice accepted rides from me, and came to my own literary readings, and invited my family and me to his annual Christmas party (characteristically, held in January, if not later…), I had the good fortune to be on his approved list.

Why I was on this list, or seemed to be, was always something of a puzzle to me. As writers, we were of divergent styles and often of widely varying philosophies. I wrote prose. He wrote mainly poetry. I prize clarity and accessibility in writing. He loved mysteries and convolutions and puzzles. Once we argued over books we liked and didn't like. There wasn't, as I recall, any common ground. I remember trying to winnow out the essential kernels of our discourse, proposing to him that while I would rather read a great story told by a mediocre writer, he would rather read just about anything by a brilliant writer. "Yes," he said with laugh and a challenging stare, and that was that.

In thinking back, I've concluded that a key thing Maurice prized in the writers he loved was suffering. He had no interest in or respect for those who aimed for commercial success or comfort. One had to bleed for one's art. The fact that I'd spent nearly thirty years of my life eking out a modest and chronically uncertain income in order to pursue my interests as a scholar and writer seemed to be my ticket into the circle of friends to which he was warmly and fiercely devoted. Maurice loved the underdog, and he loved his chosen friends. And with a vehemence that shocked me sometimes, he hated the smug, and he loathed those editors, fellow writers, and other benighted souls he saw as his enemies and as enemies of decency and truth.

I might have had one more drive with Maurice, but it was not to be. Shortly before leaving on a family trip to Australia and New Zealand, I invited him out for coffee. He was, I realize now, in his end game. We made it as far as the car. Yet the moment he settled into the passenger seat, he panicked. "I can't do it," he cried. "I can't breathe. I've got to get back to the house."

The minute that followed was terrifying for him and for me. I helped him out of the car, helped him back up the stairs to his apartment, steadied him as he fumbled for his keys, and then kept close as he snatched up a lifeline that carried oxygen from a tank.

I am happy to report that this, our final time together, had a happy ending. With his equilibrium restored, he pivoted from near helpless-ness to being, as always, the consummate host. Maurice brewed a pot of coffee and made sandwiches. Although there would be no drive this time, we had our coffee after all. We sat at his kitchen table, enjoyed the sandwiches he'd made, and swatted words and ideas back and forth like two other people might play ping pong. Mostly, as I recall, we discussed what would prove to be his final book project, a memoir that happily will be in print from SUNY Press not long after this essay is.

Then, a couple of weeks later, while Debbie, our kids, and I were on the far side of the globe, Maurice Kenny, passenger extraordinaire, breathed his last in the company of friends.

**thumbtacks**
❖ Ethan Shantie

No, it wasn't
all strawberries,
so light tobacco
already lit

in this foreign house where I touch
sweet grass
I have accepted
only as
    decoration.

There are too many letters here to sort
so I only store them.

**Moving the Village**
❖ Maurice Kenny

Running:

    Crow has called ten times:

    River waters are empty. The sun
    does not show salmon. The creek
    gags on bones of trout.
    Corn grows smaller each summer.
    Soon it will be stunted from under-nourished
    soils and kernels look ragged teeth
    in the mouths of dried witches.

    You will starve. You have not re-placed the soil.
    Nor have you allowed the doe to feed her young;
    bear complains there is no honey in the hive,
    birds are angry there are no cherries.
    All you have are holes at the wood's edge
    that stink from your feasting.

    Seekers say to dismantle your house;
    fill baskets with accoutrements, utensils,
    drums, turtle rattles,
    carry the old and lead young.
    The seekers have found a village where pine
    grows tall in unfettered air and rivers run fresh.
    Hawk soars high above berry vines and corn
    will grow, and squash. Wolf is fat.

    Thank sun for rising on this place of many birds.
    Leave tobacco on rocks. Look up and down
    and all around you; then follow and be strong:
    think of mountains north from here.
    Remember bones you leave behind
    and spirits who need meal.

    The Speakers advise you to march under stars,
    greet dawn within the new circle.
    A fire waits your pots.

## Ice Climbers Trained by Chickadees
❖ Alex French

10 miles now returning from the walls of the trap dike,
the slides of Mt. Colden
where I was thankful the clouds
wouldn't show me the valley below.

Resting beside the reclaimed Marcy Dam
with ice screws, axes, helmets,
wet, sore feet
The chief of the winter-ready birds
lands on my snowshoe
demanding trail mix for his flock.
Raised palm,
It lands on my index finger
collecting tolls of
peanuts, sunflower seeds.

They sing to us, granting safe passage.
I know you're not supposed to feed the wildlife
but we were very tired
and didn't have a choice.

## The Linden Tree
❖ Maurice Kenny

*For Anneliese Maus*

Guilty! it was placed between leaves
of Bradbury's ZEN AND THE ART
OF WRITING. I carried it out
from Germany, Berlin, after you
had answered my question: "What
is a linden tree?" You raised a glance,
then spread arms wide,
and exclaimed with smiles:
"You're standing beneath one now."
I was pleased to learn something new,
and remarked I'd carry a twig back
to America hidden between leaves
of a book. Somewhere in France
I reached for Bradbury to touch
my new linden bough acquisition.
It was gone! had dropped out
on the train between
Belgium and France.
                    Now I do
not have my keepsake of Berlin
with your smiling reference.
I'll try to keep a tighter book,
perhaps use a rubber band
next time I collect a memory.

## At the Left Bank Café, a Touch of Paris
❖ Maurice Kenny

*For Ursula Trudeau*

It would appear the lady had just arrived
from a millenary shop with her new
bonnet and what a bonnet it was: Madame
was seated at a fairly small table with friends
enjoying a divine dinner at an elegant French
Café laughing and admiring an art show they
only then had paid a visit and toured the gallery.
Her hat was stunning without a doubt: at least
a foot and inches wide; black with no veil but there
upon the top were the most feminine of flowers,
pinned surely by the household maid. Roses
could be supposed but not red or wine or crimson.
On each end of the brim striking to the galley, night
eyes stared from across the room. There a man
and woman's gaze caught her hat at either side;
the man's keen sight spotted white blooms:
two delicate somewhat bluish flowers or that is how
the pale lights shone upon her blossoms.

Under the wide brimmed hat she smiled
a pretty smile which possessed the evening.
Momentarily a young man stooped
to her and caught a charm, a smile and rudely
took the conversation from her fellow diners, one
who was telling of a tour to Turkey that summer…

The beautiful lady below the cloth roses softly
smiled and allowed the youth to continue to speak.
She smiled once again and lowered the wine to her lips.

## The Worm Dream
❖ Phil Gallos

Helen Hill has always been a place for the unexpected. It rises above the platitudes of the floodplain the way the back of a bear rises above a berry patch – snout to the north, rump toward the south, flanks sloping steeply east and west.

Perhaps the hill thought it would remain that way forever, unmolested in paradise. But the people came, and, like harvesting ants, they mowed the bear's hair – the sky-scratching pines and the resonant spruces – hauling the bounty down the hill to the sawmill at the dam old Pliny Miller had built across the river where he turned timber into lumber. Later, the lumber was hauled back to where it had once lived and assembled into houses on what, by then, had become a sheep pasture. The houses multiplied, proliferated, seemed to erupt from the bald slopes so that the hill came to resemble a bear shaved naked with a bad case of hives. Then the houses filled with people who had no part in their building and who had never expected to be sent to such a place as Saranac Lake or to hear the word tuberculosis uttered in reference to them.

If you slogged up Helen Street from the west – up from Church and Saint Bernard Streets, their several godly edifices fat with the faithful on Sundays – you might have passed the bench, the one where my grandmother paused to rest on her ascents to Franklin Avenue: a park bench without a park; a place to park oneself; a reprieve for walkers with bad lungs, to sit waiting for their breath to return from wherever it was that it went.

When the men and women who populated these houses were sent here from the mills and the mines and the warfront and the secretarial pools, those who sent them did not expect them to live – expected, instead, that they would never come home breathing; and those who were sent came expecting nothing. They knew better than to expect, but that did not keep them from hoping that the power filling the churches at the bottom of the hill would continue to fill their lungs with air. When they did not perish, when they refused to be passengers in narrow boxes loaded through the windows of the night train idling by the cold-storage vault at the edge of the cemetery on the bear's eastern hip, those whose expectations they defied expected them to return to the cities and their families and their places of labor. But many did not go, chose instead to stay and make a life where they had found life – each life a miracle, at least to its owner – and so they doubly confounded the ones who had expected them to die.

It is warm today, with a gentle breeze and a beneficent sun. I am not here because I need the rest, but I close my eyes anyway. I am sitting on the bench with a man who looks like Steve but is not Steve. The bench is at the corner of Front and Helen – not where it once was, but near enough that my grandmother could find it, though she has been dead for fifty-seven years. It is facing uphill on the corner where the Hennessy house used to be. The man who looks like Steve and I are talking, not expecting anything, when a very large worm arrives. The worm is about six feet long and ten inches in diameter. The thing about the worm that is most unexpected is that it is intelligent. It can communicate telepathically. And it has chameleon qualities. It can change its body color to match its environment.

The worm glides around and behind the bench where the ground is a mixture of grass and pavement and mulch and crushed stone. The worm goes back there; and we turn on our seats to watch. It moves over the grass, and it is green where it is over the grass; and it moves over the pavement, and the green goes to grey; and it moves over the mulch, and it becomes the color of the mulch. Then it says, "Now watch this." And it moves toward the crushed stone.

The stone is granite. Most of the pieces are about an inch in diameter; but some are larger, and they are sharp edged, and they have sharp points at the corners. There is a mixture of colors in the stone – pink and gray, a little bit of white. And there are flakes of biotite mica. They sparkle bronze in the sunlight.

The worm slides over the crushed stone; and the part of its body that is upon the stone picks up all the colors there, the white and the grey and the pink and the sparkling bronze flecks. As the worm moves, the colors and the sparkling ripple along its body. The effect is stunning, wondrous. I know that there is not another worm like this in the world; and, if there ever had been others, they are all gone.

The man who is not Steve says, "Okay. Well, watch *this*." He stands from the bench, walks to the worm and sits on the part of the worm that is resting on the crushed stone.

I jump up from the bench, walk toward the worm. I start yelling at the man who looks like Steve. "What the fuck are you doing? You're going to hurt him. Are you nuts? Get the hell off him."

So he gets off the worm and stands to the side as though appraising his work. The worm is cut and gouged where the stone had been pressed into its belly. It curls up in a ball and starts to secrete what looks like mucus onto its lacerated flesh, like a dog would lick its wounds. I figure it is trying to repair itself. I return to the bench.

The man who looks like Steve but is not Steve comes back and sits next to me again.

I say, "Jesus, look what you've done," my voice rising. "You hurt him! You hurt him bad! You just had to be an asshole. Just couldn't resist. I don't even want you around me. Get off this bench. Just get the fuck away from me!"

So he leaves.

Now a woman approaches. She looks like Sharon, but she is not Sharon. She tries to calm me. Tells me to relax, to mellow out. I get the feeling she wants to convince me that my aggravation won't change anything. She doesn't say so explicitly, but that's the message. I'm still mumbling expletives under my breath, but eventually I stop. The woman who looks like Sharon goes away.

About the same time, the man who looks like Steve returns. He is carrying a large sheet of glass and sits down on the bench. He puts the glass across our laps. We start to chat. After a while, I remember the worm; and I say, "What are you doing here? I'm not even supposed to be talking to you. And what's this glass for? It'll break, and we'll both get cut. Get it off us. Put it over there."

The man who is not Steve removes the glass. He leans it against a tree. While we're talking, another man arrives; but we don't notice. He has gone behind the bench where the worm is lying and has put the worm in a device that looks like a narrow tray made of stainless steel. We hear something behind us and turn to see what's happening there. On the side of the device are the words, "Animal Emergency Services." The man explains to us that this equipment will not replace the worm's skin, but it will warm the worm enough so that the worm's own bodily processes can heal it. When he removes the worm from the tray, though, nothing has healed. There is a big ragged wound, and the flesh is black.

The Animal Emergency Services man looks at the black hole in the worm and says, "He's not going to make it."

I plunge into a furious tirade directed at the man who looks like Steve. "You stupid worthless piece of mother-fucking shit! You just had to show how cool you are. Fucking adolescent asshole. Get away from me. I don't give a shit where you go, just go!"

I'm screaming at this point, enraged almost beyond words; wanting to cry but too angry for tears. The worm had never harmed anyone; *would* never harm anyone. It was ugly, but it was beautiful. Miraculously beautiful. And all it wanted to do was show people how beautiful it could be even though it was ugly. That's where its joy was, in surprising people with beauty where they thought there was only ugliness. And, unlike me, the worm isn't angry. It would not have counter-attacked even if it had been equipped to do so. It isn't angry; it is just hurt and dying. And it cannot understand why this happened, why anyone would want to do what the man who is not Steve had done.

The Animal Emergency Services man is gone, but the man who looks like Steve is still sitting beside me, arms crossed, blank-faced.

I stand and step away, thinking I might retch, but I'm still speaking. "You smug sonofabitch. You think you're so clever? Even a moron could understand if you sat on that creature on those rocks you'd wound it. We can foresee the future, you know, just a little bit, because we can deduce – like, if I do this bad thing, that bad thing will happen. But you can't. You're too wrapped up in your own goddamn drama."

I am in the middle of Front Street now, my fists balled at my sides, my voice hoarse from yelling. The woman who looks like Sharon but is not Sharon comes to the bench again and takes the man who looks like Steve but is not Steve by the arm and leads him away. They turn right onto Prescott Place, and then they are gone. I stand staring at the ghosts of their passing, staring toward the snout of the bear, toward the north, the direction where darkness lives, where people go when they die, and where dreams go when we awake.

Below and behind me to my left I hear wheels squeaking. Trudging up Helen Hill is a homeless man pushing a shopping cart. The cart is piled high with blue plastic bags bulging with his life. He stops, looks at the worm...looks at me. He says, "So this is the way the miraculous dies, abandoned and bleeding behind a park bench, a victim of our infantile self-involvement and our addiction to one-upmanship. We murder what is precious and irreplaceable to prove our superiority to what we cannot be."

After a pause, he says, "You look surprised? What did you expect?"

I sit down on the bench. My face feels like there are houses sprouting from it. The homeless man removes a rag from his hip pocket, blows his nose into it, sticks it back in his pocket, and resumes his noisy trek.

Something brushes across my feet. I open my eyes in time to see the shadow of my grandmother turn the corner, sliding upward toward Franklin Avenue.


**Journal Entry on a Greyhound Bus**
❖ Lance Henson

*For Maurice Kenny*


Dusk the sound of a woman softly singing
The suns warm and waning light empties the trees of their long
Shadows that spill to the ground
Leaving Memphis
Under a bridge the tarp of a sleeping homeless vet
Flaps like a thing torn from a dream
It is Sunday evening
The Mohawk kid in front of me takes a long pull
On a whiskey bottle
I watch the steady drone of headlights
The gray road whining beneath me
Hours from tomorrow
The dark trees are old men in worn coats
Watching us pass....

**Peaches on the Fridge, I Wait for You**
❖ Alex French

For three days now
I've waited
for two peaches
we found in market
to ripen.
Each morning I lift
them from atop the fridge
to see if this
will be the morning.
Each evening I press
against their firmness
measuring resistance
against incisors.
I wait patiently
for the moment when they'll
flood my mouth
run their viscous, sticky, river
down my cheeks
The sort of event
fitting of a shower,
a short nap,
I wait.


**Before Supper**
❖ Maurice Kenny

before
the fire
flaming
as gaze shifts
to the window
view autumnal
mountains'
burning
shoulders

## My Father's Shotgun
❖ Alex French

I was 7 years old
the first time
I fired that 12 gauge
in a field in Central Texas.
"Hold it tight against your shoulder"
you told me.
I closed my eyes,
squeezed the trigger
and was thrown to my back
gun uncontrolled on the ground
and you laughed and laughed.
I loved that gun
You told me it would be mine
on my 16th birthday.

When I was 12 years old
you drove off up the dirt road.
mom was screaming
I checked the closet
unable to find that favorite gun.
As I began up Butterbowl Road
she told me to stop
she looked at me
as if I was also about to die.
I found you crying in your truck
parked in the top field.
I took the loaded gun away from you
put the safety back on
so you wouldn't stick the barrel in your mouth.

When I was 13 years old
The two of you were divorcing
You sold off your guns
including that 12 gauge
You didn't have the right to sell
my gun, the one I took from you.

When I turned 16 years old
my stepfather
gave me a Remington 12 gauge
with open sights.
Though I hadn't spoken to you in two years
I wondered if you remembered
your promise.
That fall I shot a doe
that turned out to be a male fawn.
Its spine snapped in half
at 60 yards away.
he was bleating in pain
for his mother.
As I hovered over him with a second bullet
I looked up and made eye contact with her
only 20 yards away
knowing he was about to die.

Now I'm 30 years old.
The Remington sits in the corner of my bedroom
with some rust on the barrel.
I don't touch it much
I don't like the sound of it firing
It's taken so much more
than my hearing.


## In Rome
❖ Maurice Kenny

time seems to flee
at a faster rate
and the shock hits strong
when a twenty-year-old lad
takes your arm
and guides across
angry traffic

then you
realize
it is very late

**Words?**
❖ Maurice Kenny

My phone is in the right-hand pocket,
TV's off, radio sits in the kitchen
so low that I cannot hear New Orleans
blues well here in the work room.

I have not really signed the will as it
has not been finalized by my attorney. The writer,
not me, has not finished it properly.
I must this very minute find someone qualified.
Perhaps John, Carol, or Ruth!
Perhaps my father who wrote many wills,
then tore them up as failures. He was
quite determined not to die just then.

Then why do I sit here with pen in hand,
(what a classic cliché) knowing for certain
the old bod is failing to sleep this minute
before my very eyes. I am sitting with head bent,
feet twinkling, physique feeling crumbled,
absent of any recognized energy... oh! for a Coca
Cola, or coffee, black which would give
a huge lift to the arm, leg, or any part
of my body which needs a lift, hug, rub,
or squeeze, or hank to let the brain
up there know what's on down here.
That brain is so smart! It has no idea
what the heart is thinking. Or what
it is capable of doing: just simply
shutting down the motors. I realize
that that is exactly what it wishes to do.
                    EXPLODE!
And leave me in the dark of dark
without calling the family to say...
mournfully: "he has gone; left the world.
Sorry! Nothing in the till for anyone."

**time travels**
❖ Walter Hoelbling

these days
looking around the globe
one might believe that we are travelling in time

just in the wrong direction

regression as progress
seems to be
the dominant notion of the day
creating wannabees in various disguises
    populist czars, sultans, nationalists, dictators,
    assorted self-appointed snake-oil salesmen
    and saviors of their peoples' wealth and health,
trumpeting fences, walls, tough immigration laws,
etc., etc.
to keep out all those aliens

    who otherwise are welcome
    as our partners in the global trade
    that seems to dominate the world of greed

so we can all be ourselves

    whatever that might mean

claiming to solve the problems of tomorrow
    with memories of yesterday
is hopeless and quite dangerous

do you remember
what that glorified past
actually was?

**when my time comes**
❖ Walter Hoelbling

when my time comes
it comes
and I will gladly leave
to those who go on living
the task of sorting out
the mess I have accumulated
over years

let them discover
not only the stamp collection
the bank accounts
but also unknown niches
of their father's/friend's/husband's life
the words unspoken
scribbled on some paper
thoughts never shared
for lack of time or opportunity
the letters to a friend of yore
emails to many people
hints of potential
love affairs that maybe never happened
ideas to change the world
into a better place

here I am
  with the last 6 before my years
envisioning life after death

a sign of vanity
perhaps
or an expression of despair

I am not sure

it may just be
the fleeting thoughts
on a clear winter evening

when cold creeps slowly
but insistently
into your bones

reminding you

    of all that cold space
    in our universe
    how it grows larger by the second

making you wonder
if it has a plan
and if that plan
included you
speculating
about your destiny

**A Typical Adirondack Morning**
❖ Maurice Kenny

    *For Alex Aubet*

Four young whitetail doe
stagger through snow, winter
lips cold seeking apples
my thoughtful neighbors
threw out to the back yard
as two crows sat determined
but terrified, chased to sit
on the rail of my balcony
of those animals sniffing
through snow piles for fruit
and whatever else that might
be found tossed for crows
or blue jays or chickadees
who will forge elsewhere
though they will return in May
when the doe will brush
forest mosquitoes from the fur
of their fawns

## The Strawberry Man
❖ Alan Steinberg

I grew up in Bedford-Stuyvesant, and the strawberries I ate growing up were big and fat and dry as cardboard. So, to give them flavor and life, we drowned them in whipped cream and ice cream and syrup and anything else that was sweet and gooey. And then I went out to Washington and Idaho and forgot all about strawberries. After all, in Washington it was apples and cherries. And in Idaho it was, well, you guessed it – potatoes.

Then I came back east, to the North Country, to Paul Smiths and Saranac Lake. And I met Maurice – the Mohawk Poet. And he had grown up not so much on the reservation but in Brooklyn, in Crown Heights, not all that far from Bed-Stuy. And he had been out west, also, riding the Greyhound bus to places I knew in Washington and Idaho and Oregon. And so we had a lot to talk about, to reminisce about. Then one day he said to me, "Let's go pick strawberries." And my heart sank.

If I wanted to eat cardboard, being an English professor was the perfect profession. With all those boxes of books and duplicating paper stacked everywhere, I could gorge on them and never have to leave the building. Now, someone I admired greatly as a writer was asking me to go hiking up some steep dry hill, with bears and coyotes and God-knows what else lurking, to actually try and pick the cardboard berries. But how do you say *No* to someone with such a deep and resonant voice and such fierce and focused determination? So, off we went.

And halfway up this steep and sandy hill, with the snow-topped Adirondack Mountains looming in the distance, this Pulitzer-nominated Brooklyn-Mohawk poet turned to me and said, "Do you see them?" I looked around. I hoped he meant the mountains and not a pack of wolves. "Which one is Whiteface?" I asked.

He gave me a hard look – one snagged halfway between amazement and disdain. Then he shook his head, mostly in resignation. "I meant the strawberries," he said, in a surprisingly low and sad voice. And in one sudden swoop, he bent down and with his thumb and forefingers pulled up, like a chicken pecking at grain, a half-dozen or so blood-red berries each about the size of an aspirin. Then he stretched his arm out to me, palm-up, and said, "Try them."

I thought about running away. I thought about pretending I hadn't heard him. I thought about a lot of things, all mostly pathetic and cowardly. Finally, I just took a deep breath laced with resignation, took the berries and forced myself to taste them. And no, they weren't cardboard. They were on the opposite end of the universe from card-board. It was amazing: a dozen little blood-red berries oozing sweet-ness and tartness both. Years of strawberry paranoia gave way in that one brief moment to strawberry addiction. I bent to the earth. I pulled at the berries. I shoved them into my gaping mouth. I moved on, like some hunched-over, four-legged shuffling beast. And when I had finally gorged myself – or rather pulled some unused bending-muscle in my back – and forced myself to stand upright, I realized I was yards away from Maurice. And he was just standing there, arms folded, grinning. "Just remember," he said in a surprisingly gentle and sympathetic voice, "the bears like them, too."

**Strawberry Moon**
❖ Dennis Maloney

*for Maurice Kenny*

Deep in the evening
of the summer solstice
the strawberry moon hung
huge over the mountains
walking across the salt flats
illuminating them
with an iridescent glow

In June when fruit
bursts forth the Mohawk
would gather wild berries
the juice running
down their mouths
staining their tongues
and faces with joy

Poems that keep alive

these ancient songs

**Wild Strawberries**
❖ Kayla French

*For Dr. Kenny*

I did not eat wild strawberries last summer
the change came too quickly
one day the blackening snow piled by roads
and the next my son was walking
barefooted, for the first time, through tall greens
dandelions
born during the only blizzard of the season
*new year*
*a dream as fresh as falling flakes*
my toes sinking into earth to feel for the first time
a mother

I did not eat wild strawberries
but I did not lose you
just time
slipping like river through fingers spread

I suppose I should not be thinking of death
but it is April 15th, nearly Easter
and in my yard daylilies are peeking through wet earth
robins sing on still-bare boughs
and *spring is on the maple bud*
tomorrow will be one year since you died
and my son is finding his voice in words
these two things awaken in me
like opening azalea
pink, vibrant, true
awareness of mortality
so this summer
I will go *to greet and thank the wild strawberry*
I will bloody my fingers with their juice
and eat slowly
as you did riding Greyhound
I will let them roll around before mashing seeds catching teeth
they will only be up for a drop of time
I will not miss it

**Reading Ryokan**
❖ Dan Bodah

Reading Ryokan on the bus this morning,
I stopped to stare, unfocused, into the Brooklyn traffic.

I thought about Ryokan's clean, short lines,
The images like individual petals of a flower in a clear pond.

Brooklyn struck me through the window
And demanded Walt Whitman's breathlessly long lines,
Painted bright yellow along the curbs in front of endless 3rd Avenue
warehouses.

The bus turned, and I pondered Ryokan's lines and his transparency,
My eyes unfocused, letting the city outside fall
Onto the surface of the window, out there, a floating image.

I thought about Ryokan's words on striving for status and beauty,
How all is illusion. It is so much easier, it struck me,
To see the world as an illusion than to hear it as an illusion.
The grinding bus gears, the street sounds,
Are so difficult to set aside at a remove.

Now, I am home, writing this poem.
My son, in the other room, just stopped singing to himself.
What's he doing now?
It is hard to believe that all is illusion
When he calls me!

**Home**
❖ Maurice Kenny

Halfway to midnight
they met my plane
stashed my bags
and memories
in the rear of the car
and surprised by delight
the boys pulled out
a straw box of
gorgeous
ripe strawberries
and I bellied
them quickly
all the way
to Potsdam

this is the way
to finish
travels
not with exhaustion
with cool ripe fruit
offered by friends

### Židovské muzeum v Praze (Prague Jewish Museum)
❖ Maurice Kenny

We'd been hunting Kafka for days…
sun burning and street stones
fire to flip flop sandals. We found his
cemetery and stood silent in awe of this
incredible artist who had long kept
our brains to his words. His favorite
café was gone from the street, but we bought
postcards and a book or two in the Kafka shop
and spent time in the dark museum.
                                  Under
light rain we stood for tickets to the Museum
and fear rose to what we would find.
Antiquity for sure, but not expecting
Sitting Bull's name on the wall, nor Geronimo,
nor Chief Hendrick, or Roman Nose, never
Crazy Horse or Big Foot or Rain-in-the-Face.
There on the walls I saw Red Jacket, Gowane,
and name after name after name: Native
men and women who struggled against church
and government to live peacefully in their
country. Big Foot and Yellow Bird, Gladys
Bissonette, Roman Nose, and these names
went on ad infinitum.
                       For every Weitzman carved
into the walls of this ancient synagogue
there was a Rokwaho, a John Mohawk,
a Diane Decorah or Diane Burns, Ellen
Moves Camp, a Sally Benedict, a Jim Welch,
a Black Kettle. I stood at the railing shaking
in terror, sobbing in horror for the souls
behind all names, children, babes in arms
burnt in an oven or on the blade of an army
bayonet. For every Schwartz suffocating in a gas
chamber…the name written on the Temple walls
of this ancient tomb…there were Native
names painted on the buffalo robe calendars:
Pedro Bissonette – Lakota drunk in an NYC
gutter who went home to fight for his people

now sleeps in an unmarked grave at Wounded
Knee; or Chief Pontiac – assassinated
for protecting his home and children.
Manny (Papago) – shot on Tucson bar steps
by seven white boys who don't like Indians
or Jews, or Blacks or Gays or Chinks
or big noses, small feet or rich
lands, or poems by Peter Blue Cloud,
or Hillary Cooper's beautiful wife who
escaped Auschwitz to the Adirondacks:
Ginsberg, Levertov, Steinberg, Hauser…
names etched into books of the century's
horror, madness; names like Little Belly,
Young King, Phillip Deere…oh! glory, hundreds
of thousands, millions remembered,
ignored, wiped from the earth: Loveman
or Lorne Simon.

                       I stood at the rail
angry, ashamed of what humans have
inflicted on their own species; hate
wasted when love and understanding
is infinitely less expensive. Huxley's
Roman Circus prevails, Kafka's world
we should fear, Hitler and Custer stand
on corners of every city, each town
flourishing in this wide world.
Jesus, even though you may not be the son
of God we welcome you back to earth.

When I was a mere boy of nine I chased
ice trucks for slivers of ice on hot
afternoons, lagged behind fruit/vegetable
wagons hoping I might grab a grape/berry.
One of my favorite games to play was follow
Ol' Sam's (he had no other names but Ol'
and Sam) rag wagon as he sullenly shouted:
"Ol' rags, ol' shoes, ol' black suits." My mom
always thought he was a gypsy and would
steal us and drag us into the rags, later
sell us. Oh little do we know of other folks.

Recently I re-read Orwell's famous blast,
warning of the future to come. It came!
Waits here among us. Huxley's
Circus is stronger and "soma" has worked
its way into every brain and dream,
the sheer thought of which should be
a nightmare as the merry-go-round
whirls and whirls us into blindness.

I shall weep for the Jew
and I shall weep for the Native,
and all the poor bastards, peoples
hated and slaughtered. I shall weep
for Lazarus as I weep for Black Elk,
Audre Lorde, and the young Chinese
student who faced the tank.

I shall continue until my day
is dark and my night is new
with moon. For we shall suffer
and I shall weep for us all.

**Bowler Hat with Collie**
**(Photo, ca. 1906-08)**
❖ Maurice Kenny

*In Prague*

You look pretty spiffy in the photo;
you look happy as well as if you had
a long-haired friend at last. You're young,
though a half-smile, but it is a smile,
suggests something good just
happened, about to make you
pleased. From what I know
that was pretty rare. I'm delighted to
see a happy smile on your lips.

**Bear Ends the First Summer on Her Own**
❖ Stephanie Coyne DeGhett

Late August.  Her dark shape a lichened rock that has learned to
move through woods.  Her footsteps quietly crush moss, wild lily-

of-the-valley.  Snapping twigs, breathy snorts and she emerges
at the woods' edge, rises to survey a swath of Queen Anne's lace,

a spread of goldenrod, a pond.  Rises to catch the scent of all around
her.  Her presence changes everything.  Landscape with bear.

She finds chokecherries, rakes shrubby wild rosebushes closer with
her claws, delicately plucks their plump red hips. The roses' leaves

have gone golden and the pond is a mirror.  Short bound, splashing
wade.  Fur spiky and glistening, the bear's dark form reflects

below her.  Twin images of bear and bear shake themselves: the
spray glitters diamonds in the beam of the sinking sun. She squints

and the soft funnel of her rounded ear gathers in late season
mosquito song, drone of flower-waddling bee, thrum of cicada,

the call of the end of summer.  Shadows of trees stripe an old tote
road.  Bear adds her traveling boulder-shadow, moves past

moosewood, witch-hobble, pine, spruce, dives off through ferns,
crashes through underbrush toward winter, towards dreams

a lichened rock might dream: the scent of wild leek swelling
below ground in spring, the call of the white-throated sparrow.

**Eli, a Story/Poem**
❖ Maurice Kenny

There was a dog
  who once was lost
  somehow.

Perhaps he jumped
  from a car
  somehow;

or maybe he was pushed
  from the car
  somehow.

This canine limped
  through traffic
  on what appeared
  a broken leg.

However he found
  himself
  in dirty streets

in NYC's Bronx
  alone,
  hungry.

He wandered many by-ways,
  many cold avenues
  in great hunger.

Sometimes boys threw
  stones at him
  or kicked him hard,

but this dog kept padding
  those Bronx streets
  knowing something good
  was there,

and one day soon he
  would find food and
  not just pizza crusts.

Days passed but like empty
  faces of people
  his dropped in sorrow.

Once he found a chicken bone,
  and he heard a little boy
  cry: "Mama, can I take him home?"

Mama looked at his scruffy fur,
  grabbed the boy's hand
  and hurried off to Macy's

as surely this dog was dirty
  hungry, mangy,
  wanted by no one.

Then one very bright morning
  after he had slept the night
  in a trashy alleyway,

he woke to sight sunshine
  and heard faint barking
  of dogs blocks away.

Naturally, if dogs can smile,
  he smiled and started off
  to find the happy dogs.

Took him a time to get there;
  sight, sound and smell
  led him from corner to corner.

Finally the barking grew louder
  yes, very much louder,
  and dog smell grew stronger.

He looked up at a building
  but as he could not read
  he did not notice the sign

on the huge building's edifice
  read ASPCA.
  The door stood closed.

He stared at the facade
  where the barking was louder,
  dog smells stronger.

He thought and thought
  and suddenly the door
  sprung open and our dog

did not hesitate one single
  moment but pranced
  through the open portal

wagging his hefty tail, flashing
   his bright eyes, drooling
   down his chops.

He just might have found
   new friends here
   in the Bronx.

The attendants
   welcomed him openly,
   though one guy said:

"Don't really know if we
   can keep him as
   we're short on food."

Just then a very pretty lady
   stepped up and said:
   I live in the North Country.

I'll just take him home with me."
   And our dog was washed,
   nails clipped, fed, medicated

and this shepherd was no longer lost,
   but drove North to the St. Lawrence
   Valley where he lived

most happily with this lovely
   lady who had a large heart...
   day and night, night and day.

Then something dreadful happened!
   she had to leave the North;
   she had to travel to Paris
   and could not take him with her;

was not allowed to travel with him.
   What would he do now ?
   But...she had a solid friend,

a man who liked dogs very much,
  and so this dog moved
  into his house.

He was very happy, warm and fed,
  exercised, followed by
    a black dog with the funny name of Gogol

and a beautiful black-and-white cat
  whose name no one can remember,
  but a lovely cat anyhow.

Each morning he raced
  with his new friends,
  chased sticks, swam rivers,

took great care in shaking
  rain water off after walks
  and dashed back home

for a good breakfast...
  happily wagging
  his heavy tail, of course.

      ...

There our shepherd lived happily
  for many, many years
  until he heard he
                    dogs barking
in the distance
      and off he went
      to find them.

**Almost a Sonnet**
❖ Maurice Kenny

*For Nick Spengler*

I, too, love Jackson Pollock;
I, too, and mad, mad;
Crashed on dirt roads
Under crab apple boughs
With a bottle of vodka…
            or course with a twist.

I, too, dropped by dreams
On paper canvas;
My crazed days like
Hopkins or Moses or Bartók
Onto the canvas of bitter sighs,
The walls of a Mexican jail.

I, too, love Jackson Pollock
Wild as a duped Hatter,
As Alice attempts to climb
From his furry hat & the dark.
Yes, I repeat, I too am mad, mad
            as Crazy Horse who was not.
More mad, mad to haunt the world
as light shines on bitten walls.

**A Voice for Native People:**
**Memories of Maurice Kenny**
❖ Joe Bruchac

I first encountered Maurice Kenny – and his formidable personality – through the mail. It was in the early years of *The Greenfield Review*, the poetry magazine I edited and published from 1970 to 1981. I'm not sure how Maurice heard of the magazine, but he sent me a submission of several poems. I liked them, but had already filled the upcoming issue and I was trying not to keep people waiting too long before publishing their work. So I returned them with a note saying that I liked them but was out of space. A few months later, a larger batch of poems arrived from him – but I was still backlogged and sent them back with regrets – adding that they were memorable and highly publishable. (So memorable, in fact, that I still remember their titles – such as "Coyote Always Followed the Old Cheyenne" – and saw every one of them eventually published elsewhere).

This time I didn't have to wait a few months for another submission. Three weeks later, a third batch of poems arrived accompanied by a letter.

"It has been my experience," the letter read, "that any magazine that rejects me three times is never going to accept anything from me. So this is probably the last time I will ever send anything to you!"

To this day I do not believe it was meant to pressure me into publishing him. It was simply a reflection of his straightforward, no-nonsense approach to his writing, his work as an editor, and his life in general. You could always count on honesty from him. I admired that – and I (having worked through my backlog) accepted two poems from that third batch.

It was, to quote from the classic film *Casablanca*, "the beginning of a beautiful friendship." Over the next four decades I would not only publish Maurice's work many times, Maurice would also include my own poems in his magazine *Contact/II*, as well as in more than one of the anthologies he edited. It was never a "tit for tat" relationship, buddies publishing each other, but a situation in which two poet-editors admired each other's work for its own merits.

Though Maurice would be known for his support – in many ways – of other writers, I am certain he never published anyone just because they were friends. His taste and his ability to spot talent was evident in each new issue of *Contact/II* and every chapbook and broadside he brought out from Strawberry Press. He was – though he liked portraying himself as uncaring and a curmudgeon, saying such things as "You wouldn't like me if you really knew me!" – a person who felt deeply about others and was always culturally sensitive. He truly was, in his own writing in which he sometimes took on the persona of such past figures in Mohawk history as Molly Brant, and in his work as an editor and then a teacher, devoted to the truth of Native history.

One example of that sensitivity was the name of his publishing company – Strawberry Press. Few may know that his original intention, which he discussed with me, was to call it Orenda Press. But Maurice decided, after listening to the reactions of Mohawk friends, that using the name orenda – which refers to the spiritual power found in all beings and things – would be inappropriate.

Strawberry Press was, by the way, a great choice. It reflected Maurice himself in so many ways. Wild strawberries are the first fruit and Maurice was one of the first Native American poets to appear in the blossoming of Native American writing that began in the late 1960s. Maurice loved strawberries – and wrote about them memorably in his poetry. It is also said that in the Sky Land, where we go after we leave this earth, the strawberries are always ripe. A common remark made by Haudenosaunee people when they recover from a serious illness is "I almost tasted strawberries."

As I've mentioned elsewhere – in a brief tribute to Maurice in *Dawnland Voices 2.0* – that is something Maurice said on a number of occasions.  Beginning with his triple (or was it quadruple?) bypass surgery more than forty years ago, Maurice gave Sula his cat a run for her money in terms of having the proverbial nine lives. He made a living out of almost dying and then resurrecting himself. Four times that I know of during the decades of our friendship.

Not that near-mortality ever held him back. I cannot number the times when Maurice and I were doing a reading or book fair in New York and Maurice was lugging a load of books – many of them by other writers whose work he was publishing and promoting, such as Diane Burns's wonderful chapbook *Riding The One-Eyed Ford* – that would have broken the back of a mule.

"I've got a free arm," I'd say. "Let me help."

"NO! I've got this," was his usual reply. Even though he had sweat on his brow and looked ready to keel over. No turtle was more stubborn than he.

I know of few writers who traveled this nation more than Maurice did. And he was stubborn about how he went about that, too. He refused to fly or get a driver's license. His first choice, as far as mode of transport went, was the bus, a choice echoed by the title of his book *Greyhounding This America*. I suspect no one knew the Port Authority bus terminal in Manhattan better than he did.

In the early years of our friendship, Maurice seemed so at home in the megalopolis that – despite his peripatetic nature – it was hard to imagine him settling down anywhere else. Little did I know that the fourth act of his life would take place in the North Country of New York State. According to Maurice, what drove him to that epic relocation was another near-death experience – being brutally mugged as he was going upstairs to his own apartment in Brooklyn.

The next thing I knew, he was in Saranac Lake teaching at North Country Community College and then later at Paul Smith's. And though his travels continued to take him far and wide across the continent – it was where he would always return for the rest of his life.

It shouldn't have surprised me. Maurice felt most connected to the Mohawk community of Akwesasne on the St. Lawrence River a bit further north than Saranac Lake and to the prodigiously talented Fadden family in the nearby tiny hamlet of Onchiota where Tehanetorens (Ray Fadden) founded, built, and ran the independent and iconoclastic Six Nations Museum. It's hard to name a contemporary Mohawk artist, writer, or leader who was not influenced in some way by Ray Fadden. And John Kahionhes Fadden – Ray's son, who taught art in the Saranac Lake High School – was the artist Maurice turned to most often for book covers and illustrations for his own work and that of others he published.

As a teacher, Maurice was memorable and beloved. That is not my independent conclusion, but the consensus of hundreds of students he taught over the years. Whenever I met anyone – native or non-native – who'd had him as an instructor the words "wonderful," "caring," and "inspiring" were most often spoken. He was also good at delivering a kick in the butt when needed. He never tolerated laziness or phoning it in from his students.

At one point, his teaching took him further afield to the University of Oklahoma, where he was equally well-received as a visiting teacher. It even led Maurice – who'd expressed disdain for contact sports in the past – to become a rabid fan of the Oklahoma football team, because some of his students were football players. While living in Norman, he hardly missed a game, sitting in the stands to root on his guys.

That connection to Norman was, in part, due to an event that Maurice played an integral part in planning – the 1992 Returning the Gift Festival at the University of Oklahoma that brought together over 300 Native American writers and storytellers from North, Central, and South America. Maurice was an original member of the steering committee and hosted one of our most important planning meetings at North Country Community College.

One of the last events I shared with Maurice was the March 2013 Native Innovation, Indigenous Poetry in the 21st Century event held at Poets House in New York. He was, quite literally, the elder spokesman of Native writing at that event. His voice no less strong than it had been four decades earlier, he was shown the sort of respect, deference, and gratitude that he deserved for his long career as poet, editor, and teacher. He also, to be honest, looked almost exactly as he did when I first met him. Maurice never seemed to age, but always looked like an elder.

There are two other things I want to address about my late friend, whose body now belongs to the earth, but whose words now belong to the generations.

The first is his place in the Native community in general and the Mohawk nation in particular. Like many of us, Maurice's ancestry was mixed. His mother was not Mohawk – though she had Seneca ancestry. Among the six nations of the Iroquois, the tradition is that you belong to the clan of your mother. Thus, if your mother is not Mohawk, you are not Mohawk. This led, on at least one occasion, to the Akwesasne tribal leadership stating publicly that Maurice Kenny was not a Mohawk. Without passing judgment, all I can say is that Maurice was who he was. He made no secret about it and gave his heart and spirit to the Haudenosaunee nation in his writing and his deeds. I have no doubt that is how he and his work will be judged by scholars and readers in the years to come. He also dealt with this divide directly in his poems, most prominently in "Going Home," which refers to his father choosing to settle his family away from the rez. The poignant last lines say it all:

> home to a Nation, Mohawk
> to faces I did not know
> and hands which did not recognize me
> to names and doors
> my father shut.

The second is his voice – both as it was spoken, declaimed in fact, and as it was written. Maurice's voice was lyric. If you read his poems aloud, they come even more alive. And his delivery was bardic. When Maurice Kenny stood to declaim his poems, that pale little man with the white pony tail seemed to grow to the stature of a giant. His voice – and what a voice it was! – could rumble like thunder, strike like lightning, soothe you like a lullaby, or move you to tears.

Whenever we read together, I always went first – with a smile on my face. Anyone who knew Maurice's delivery and had any sense would never choose to have him be the leading act. On three separate occasions, I watched what happened when a "more important" poet did not listen to what Maurice recommended before they took to the stage.

"You really do not want me to go first," he would say in all sincerity.

"Really."

"No, I am the featured reader."

"Allll riggghhht."

And then later, as Maurice was walking off the stage to thunderous applause, hearing that self-important poet say, in despair, "How can I follow that?"

Sadly, there is no good way to follow Maurice Kenny. As his friend and as a critic, the best I can do now that he's left us physically is to direct people to his work. And to tell them to be prepared to be moved, shaken, and taken on a journey they'll not soon forget by a true voice for Native people.

**Tribute**
❖ John Radigan

*For Maurice*

One by one,
year by year,
you welcomed us
aboard the war-canoe
of your life,
its gunwales stained with strong coffee
and wild strawberry juice,
a fierce black bear painted on the prow,
powerful totem,
terror of the incompetent.

Enthroned in the stern,
helmsman extraordinaire,
you tirelessly steered us
into untamed landscapes
we never would have discovered
on our own:
forgotten settlements with unpronounceable Mohawk names,
funky Brooklyn bookstores haunted by celebrities,
gritty terminals reeking of Greyhound exhaust,
runways quivering with the scream of jets
landing in Prague and Berlin.
You opened whole worlds to us,
universes swarming with frybread,
rifles, guitars, stomp dances,
Mexican painters, obnoxious Parisians.

You kept insisting that we all
grab paddles and join in.
Badgering, scolding, pleading,
you taught us the strokes,
showed us by example
just how to wield them
as we shot poetry's roaring rapids together

how to dip them, just so,
in the quieter eddies of book reviews,
and reflective pools of essay and memoir.

Your passionate generosity knew no bounds –
help, encouragement, invitations to lunch,
shelter for those in need, support of struggling artists,
gala holiday parties brimming over
with laughter and waves of cookbooks –
all flowed out from you like the warm scent
of your basil and tomato plants
in high summer.

One spring afternoon your great canoe
still driving forward at full speed
ran aground on the cold white beach
of a hospital bed,
pitching us off our seats,
leaving us dazed and disoriented
by the sudden quiet.
In the confusion, you somehow disappeared
and have not been seen since.
Your bewildered daypack, left behind
for the first time any of us could remember,
told us this was serious.

For a long time we have mourned you
as a tongue obsessively mourns
a newly-missing tooth.
But the paddles you bequeathed us
are still in our hands,
and after all these years your lessons in seamanship
have become second nature to us.

The fatal crash that split your canoe
like a milkweed pod
released us to float out,
whole fleets of us,
over the barren fields of this country and the world,
all of us carrying on the wind

something of your indomitable spirit
which will live on and on
in countless iterations
through us.

Blessings, best of friends.
Oneh.

**winter gloves in the lost and found**
❖ Ethan Shantie

after 3 am
waiting for sunlight to bisect the
window where in morning I will
watch, warm
the breeze casually brushing fir
branches across glass and back
again,
smoke rising from chimney,
slight panic at the sweet smell.
without fair permission, hear
Music forgotten and fit for milk
cartons - singing saw
whisper me to sleep
where I remember ten years gone,
someday twenty,
a room with posters and dry erase
markers marking a score
insignificant now –
perplexing then.
missed calls from numbers I don't
know and
won't redial
a debt that will remain uncollected
or an old friend
Who will ask why we let each other
become old at all.

**Looking the Truth in the Eye**
❖ Renée Sadhana

Looking the truth in the eye is a scary thing.
Looking the truth in the eye is a necessary thing.
Not looking the truth in the eye is a cowardly thing.
Yet looking the truth in the eye is a foolish thing.
Because having looked it in the eye once,
it never ever goes away again.
Ever.

Looking the truth in the eye hurts.
Looking the truth in the eye reveals things. Ugly things. Horrible
things.
Unspeakable things.
Looking the truth in the eye is a naïve thing.
Yet not knowing the truth is a wicked thing.
Not being able to look the truth in the eye is an unbearable thing.
Because you look and look – and the only thing you see
is a big fat question mark. Leaving you
empty.

Looking the truth in the eye –
Looking the truth in the eye –
Looking the truth in the eye real hard –
Things are unconcealed. Things are unshrouded. Locks are broken up.
Barriers are traversed. Borders are blown up.
Some get hurt. Some can't look.
Some are cause. Some are victim
of the situation.
Some are left alone
looking.

Looking the truth in the eye – who do you turn to?
Looking the truth in the eye – where do you go for shelter?
Looking the truth in the eye – can you bear that burden? For life?
Looking the truth in the eye – what will you do with the truth,
that is finally yours?
Do you hide it?
Do you write it and burn it up?
Do you burry it deep down inside you –
and let it eat you up alive?
Or do you tell? Tell it all? – To the trees. To the wind. To the fish. To the
rocks. To the mountains. To the flowers. To the rivers. To the oceans. To
yourself. To others?
Share? Share…
Make it even more real?

How can it do more damage? Concealed or shared?
How can I prevent it
from ever happening again?
How can I
heal?

Looking the truth straight in the eye.
Looking the truth deep in the eye.
Sharing that truth
that is now mine.

**from *The Futures***
❖ Chad Sweeney

or every thousand years God will say one thing

and the mouths of uranium mines
spill their quantum of darkness

a family tumble from an onion truck
and the onions all over the road
will form a new constellation
among the day stars of New Mexico

and the ghost of a child will return to Acoma
to bury herself among her mother's bones

to relearn the names

of coyote and crow the arroyos
where she played hide and seek with time
 changing from rabbit
to brush fire        to sandstone

and we'll all be part of her game

or you will drive across Utah

in your sleep, crossing bridges
where there are no bridges

the wheels shedding sparks, radio signals
holding you up

a bronze sculpture of night
fit against the desert

the mountains no more than wind

a wind of stones in the mouth of God

the stones He uses to chew on us

the futures
shining out from your headlights

and we will touch like that
five minutes deep

our voices petalled
the water of moving toward us

sipping fire prismatic
the taste of one hour deep the wind

nested in our mouths the words thin
light strings too long to measure

streaming from us streaming

into us the horses driven into the river
the bugle blowing death the sun

on collar bones of Sand Creek the
handlebars of a Schwinn

in the drugstore window
listening to a shadow one century wide

where Monahsetah will birth a secret
and memory plant a prophecy into the pasts

and the small of our lives will shine
as gardens for gods

our feet in moccasins the gesture of our wrists
above the coffee pot the watering can

poised over tomato vines the clay the nails
the bowls the nets the rope factory when it rains

over Nepal our scarves

releasing outward as beautipossible
narratives the nebula to read our passage

in the atoms of our hair

or you will wake in a parking lot
to watch sound drift up from the cars

to reposition your bottles
and lonely for her there

in the window chewing her bread
a maple grove in her distance, a deck of cards

in her distance

you'll sneak in to eat sugar packets, you'll
be roughly thrown out

and moments later, one ear
to the pavement

you'll hear the memory of your grandma
strike the snake with a shovel shouting *Die!*

*Satan!*
and you'll feel sorry for the shovel

The House Cat
    cries in the night,
Unafraid she
    wanders the rooms
Seeking what may
    be there
As she cries.
Is it from joy
Is it from fear
Is it from loneliness.
Each night she cries
        Perhaps it is joy

## The House Cat Cries in the Night
❖ Maurice Kenny

The house cat
        cries in the night
Unafraid she
        wanders the rooms
Seeking what may
        be there
As she cries
        Is it from joy
        Is it from fear
        Is it from loneliness
Each night she cries
        Perhaps it is joy

**Headman**
❖ Stephen Lewandowski

In those days
if you said
you lost your head
it meant no hissy fit,
you completely lost your head
and the barbarians wrapped it
carefully in some rich cloth
to take home.

They had some ideas about
what your head could become.
The skull was, as they say,
emptied and scrubbed clean,
then gilded by metalsmiths and
trimmed by jewelers
with precious stones.

Your skull became
a cup for
spilling libations or
drinking toasts at
ceremonies to praise,
feed or propitiate the gods.
When they drank,
it would be
had you lips left
a kiss.

*With thanks to Livy*

**I Swear**
❖ Stephen Lewandowski

1.
Two lovers are ogling each other over
the Salvation Army's checkout counter.
I can tell they are deeply smitten from the way
they look at each other long and warm as if
they are already home in bed.
Jeez, I am jealous. They buy three plates,
two of one pattern and one of another.
Looks like someone's coming to dinner.
They pay less than $3 and meander away
hand in hand up the street with
their purchase slung in a plastic bag.
If they own only these goods
at least they have one another.
Now, among the racks, shelves and bins
of discarded goods can I remember
what I came here for?

2.
Walking down Main Street, I hear
this guy back of me on his cellphone
oblivious to the rest of the world
and slow down to get the full story.
He passes me and I see
he's dressed entirely in black and old style—
the crotch of pants somewhere down his thighs
causing an odd ballooning and deflating action
as he goes. I'm listening now to his rap
which includes frequent interjections
of "fuck" and "fucking" as if
his "fuck" is just the equivalent of
"you know," you know. The call
must be to a friend or maybe an attorney
to whom he is explaining the fine points
of a domestic violence case.

I don't know what he pays for service but
minus all the "fucks" and "fucking," I bet
he'd save a bundle. Now he turns aside and
crosses the street but I can hear him as he goes.
Halfway across he fades but undoubtedly
some other citizen will soon pick up his signal.

3.
Their quiet blessings and
his unthinking curses
ring through the universe.


**Barcelona Shop**
**(Possibly a Confusion of Tongues)**
❖ Maurice Kenny

I'm not sure the woman of the shop
under thick lip-stick smiles was
trying to sell me the toy flamenco doll
or her eighteen-year-old son. She
kept talking *palabras* to me I did
not grasp, but the youth, handsome
that he surely was, translated
in slurred English, as though nervous
he confessed he wanted
to go to America to study ballet,
but when I asked why, and that there
is a great ballet company in Spain,
he merely smiled and hung his head.
Ashamed he looked to *mamacita*
who physically pushed him closer
as he tried to hide behind the counter
where hung t-shirts stamped "I Love
Barcelona" and another with a black
bull painted on scarlet cloth.

I don't believe he wanted to be
a dancer, nor coquette, nor was
*la señora* sure of what she meant.
A mere confusion of tongues.

**Arrowhead, part II**
❖ Ethan Shantie

In my bedroom at night,
my throat is the sound of birds chirping.
You're in a hospital bed and though we
refuse to cash in our chips
maybe this is the first step on a
short walk
home for you.

Please don't go.
Please do not let my last image of you
be a hospital bed.

Your pony tail has already been replaced
by the tug of an oxygen
tube, which kept you confined inside
this last year,
away from your strawberries, which you replaced
with vitamins and pills whose labels you could not read.

Your study overlooks a dirt parking lot.

Christ,
my Arrowhead,

have we been friends through three homes already?
Now four, with the nurse making rounds each hour.

I have taken eight of your eighty-six years and that
has passed with the swiftness of our first handshake.

Arrowhead,
if you must go, don't linger.
But don't either meet your parents
at the clearing at the end of the path.
I am not ready. I want to become nothing with you.

Your phone goes to voicemail.

Your cat has stopped eating.

In your unsigned will you left me
your collection of Faulkner books
but who the fuck am I supposed to
talk about them with?

Who else will chide me for a love
of pop
and pop authors?

Who else will recite love affairs at the dinner table
over cup after cup of percolated coffee?

They want you to cut chapters from
your autobiography and you're doing that work
exactly
from a hospital bed.

Hear the birds,
Hear the drunk ramblings in a letter I never sent –

If you must go, please become nothing.


**silence**
❖ Walter Hoelbling

when we hear the silence
in our closed eyes
direct it into our soul
let it conclude its work
become our consciousness

far from the world's noise
if only for moments
in secret    with no audience
we become one
with nature quietly shaping our lives

**Confess**
❖ Maurice Kenny

My mirror is great to talk with.
It doesn't really have any answers,
but it doesn't ignore you the way
the rest of the world closes ears
and eyes, I might add. And as I brush
my teeth you can't argue with
mirrors either. Just stare blankly.
No harm is done, no threat to anyone.

It may cause a bite of chilled laughter,
or a salty tear drop to puckered lip.
But you can trust the mirror will not
betray your happiness as you sometimes sing Holiday's blues, or cry,
or throw my shaving brush against a wall.
It is a valued friend those morns
when you need a friend most
after three mugs of steaming coffee
or after lonely nights at a favorite bar.

**I Never Thought of Death When Young**
❖ Maurice Kenny

I never thought of death
      when young
Now each time I touch
      a sharp knife
Its coldness, sharpness
      speaks
Each time I swallow aspirins
      I seem to drown
      in the glass of water.

It is a companion
      Pale cat
      Dog I've never touched
      Fish swimming in a globe

When young I never
      thought of the need
      to die
            alone
            or in a crash
A knife was welcome
      had no fear
      did not need a cat

Now, yes, now my companion
      is fear

I never thought of death
when young.
now each time I touch
a sharpe knife
it coldness, sharpness
speaks
each time I swallow aspirins
I seem to drown
in the glass of water

it is a companion
the cat
dog I have never touched
fish swimming in a globe

when young I never
thought of the need
to die
a have
or in a crash
a knife was welcome
had no fear.
did not need a cat
now, yes, now my companion
is fear.

## After You Died, Poet of the Mohawk Nation
❖ Danicla Gioseffi

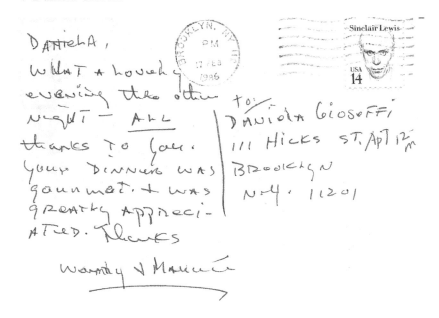

I found your old *thank you* note,
complimenting one of the dinners
I'd long ago served you –
when we were neighbors across Clark St.
from each other in the 1980's of Brooklyn Heights.

We were young poets in teeming New York City then.
The last time I saw you at Poets House, New York
was at a Native American Poetry Conference
organized by our Abenaki friend Joe Bruchac.

You were the most exciting reader that day,
emotionally strong, clear as a spring sky,
blue as your Irish eyes still smiling brightly.
You kindly said I was "still beautiful"
though I was an aged seventy-three.

We talked and laughed as old friends do.
We took a happy photo together, both of us elderly,
facing a narrowing road ahead that could end soon
in the approaching arms of death. You rest in a peace

beyond knowing in the distance ahead of me. How good
to remember our times on Clark St. sharing poems,
gossiping about the nepotisms on the poetry scene.

The lunches and dinners we shared, Dear Friend.
You always busy editing *Contact/II*.  Me,
busy writing and raising my daughter
after a sad divorce you befriended me through.
I wrote many book reviews for you.
We went on to publish many books since then, too.

Your poems of the Adirondacks woods,
fishing their steams, exploring their meadows
and fields, berry picking, capturing their wildlife
and the flavor of your father's Mohawk roots,
writing of the Native American experience,
in your works validating indigenous
culture and history. Both of us excoriating
the brutal turbo-capitalist processes that pillage
our blessed Earth. We helped pioneer the burgeoning
of multicultural literature, Comrades in Arms,
with our weaponry, verses, extolling nature's

glorious bounty. Traveling from The North Country,
giving readings, offering prophetic Mohawk oratory
in bookstores, coffeehouses, tribal venues,
giving as many performances as a hundred or more
a year. You'd survived terrible abuse from strangers
and the grief of your parents' divorce. You knew the
landscape of many lands from Butler University in Indianapolis
to Mexico, the Virgin Islands, and Chicago,
before we met in New York City. You moved back
to the North Country Adirondacks of your youth, but
you're not really dead anywhere, Maurice.

You live on like a blue bird singing poetry
in my memory, Maurice. You glow on in our spirits,
clear as a sunny day or the North Star. I hear your voice,
Maurice, I still hear it resonating truth.
Poet of the Mohawk Nation,

You live on like singing in my memory.
I hear your voice, Maurice of the Mohawk Nation.
in your resonant tone. You're still
*Dancing Back Strong the Nation.* You're riding onward
*Greyhounding This America,* you're summering
among the bears, you're haunting the woods
of Saranac Lake. Your words still reverberate
in the cries of the hawk, eagle, and drum.

You're still giving us hope that America
will understand the wisdom of our native peoples
in their wise communion with our only planet home,
our faltering, our beleaguered,
our blessed, Mother Earth.

**Last Will and Testament**
❖ Maurice Kenny

I watched my dad
change it from day to day:
Monday he would be mad
at my step-mother...change;
Tuesday he'd be mad at my
sisters and their husbands...change;
and every day he was furiously
angry with me as I would not
get out of bed at six on a
Saturday am to fix tires
on some guy's Ford.
High School was rough enough...
I didn't need that hassle.
Well, he'd get up and change...
the will...not always in my favor.

Different day now!
With help from Dan, my attorney,
I'm attempting to write my will...
and guess what... I keep changing it...
almost daily! Guess why?

**The Height of Ego**
❖ Maurice Kenny

I cannot
            conceive
                        of the world

    without me.

Dan remembers me saying this.

## Books by Maurice Kenny

*The Hopeless Kill* (1956)
*Dead Letters Sent, and Other Poems* (1958)
*With Love to Lesbia* (1959)
*And Grieve, Lesbia* (1960)
*North: Poems of Home* (1977)
*Only As Far As Brooklyn* (1979)
*I Am The Sun* (1979)
*Dancing Back Strong the Nation: Poems by Maurice Kenny* (1981)
*Kneading the Blood* (1981)
*Blackrobe: Isaac Jogues, b. March 11, 1607, d. October 18, 1646: Poems* (1982)
*Boston Tea Party* (1982)
*The Smell of Slaughter* (1982)
*Wounds Beneath the Flesh* (1983)
*The Mama Poems* (1984)
*Is Summer This Bear* (1985)
*Between Two Rivers: Selected Poems, 1956-1984* (1985)
*Greyhounding This America* (1988)
*Humors And/Or Not So Humorous* (1988)
*The Short and the Long of It* (1990)
*Last Mornings in Brooklyn* Press (1991)
*Rain and Other Fictions* (1991)
*Tekonwatonti: Molly Brant (1735-1795): Poems of War* (1992)
*On Second Thought: A Compilation* (1995)
*Backward to Forward: Prose Pieces* (1997)
*In the Time of the Present: New Poems* (2000)
*Tortured Skins and Other Fictions* (2000)
*Carving Hawk: New and Selected Poems 1956-2000* (2005)
*Connotations* (2008)
*Feeding Bears* (2010)
*Perplexed: Early Poems, 1958-1974* (2015)
*Saranac Lake Ghost Poems* (2016)
*Monahsetah, Resistance, and Other Markings on Turtle's Back* (2017)
*Angry Rain: A Memoir* (2018)

…and still more to come.